Linn's
Philatelic Gems 4

Philatelic Gems 4 presents seldom-told stories behind some of stampdom's most fascinating, yet lesser-known rarities. These stamps cover the length and breadth of the world. *Philatelic Gems 4*, like its predecessors, not only tells stories of 19th-century rarities but also presents modern gems that have been on sale at post offices within the past 20 years.

Welcome to the continuing romance and mystery of *Philatelic Gems 4*.
by
Donna O'Keefe

Published by *Linn's Stamp News*, the world's largest and most informative stamp newspaper, Post Office Box 29, Sidney, Ohio 45365. *Linn's* is a division of Amos Press, Inc., which also owns Scott Publishing Company, publishers of *Scott Stamp Monthly* and the Scott line of stamp catalogs, albums and mounts.

Copyright 1989 by Amos Press, Inc.

033058   Library of Congress Catalog Number 84-230765

In Grateful Appreciation . . .

I wish to thank these stamp collectors and dealers who helped make *Philatelic Gems 4* a reality:

> Alan Benjamin
> Torbjorn Bjork
> Joel L. Bromberg
> David Feldman
> John Griffiths
> Keith Harmer
> Edgar A. Hirdler
> Virginia Horn
> George Holschauer
> Susan Hughes
> Roxane Leckey
> Edwin Lindenfeld
> Robson Lowe
> Walter Mader
> William E. Mooz
> Michael Rogers
> Peter Robertson
> F. Burton Sellers
> Robert A. Siegel
> Gordon H. Torrey
> Herbert A. Trenchard
> Scott Trepel
> L.N. Williams
> Dragomir Zagorsky

Donna O'Keefe

Contents

INTRODUCTION.	vii
AUSTRALIA	
1915-24 2½-penny missing numerator	1
1932-33 6-penny inverted overprint	3
AUSTRIA	
Lombardy-Venetia 1858 newspaper tax stamps	5
BANGKOK	
1885 32¢-on-2-anna "B" overprint	7
BELGIAN CONGO	
1898 10-franc inverted center	9
BERMUDA	
1874 3-penny-on-1d provisional	12
BOLIVIA	
1924 10-centavo airmail invert	15
BRAZIL	
1843 Pack strip	17
BRITISH SOLOMON ISLANDS	
1939-51 2½-penny imperforate between	19
BULGARIA	
1879 25-centime imperforate	21
1882 5-stotinka error of color	23
BUSHIRE	
1915 5-kran inverted overprint	25
CAPE OF GOOD HOPE	
1900 Baden-Powell issues.	27
CHINA	
1897 2¢-on-3-candareen doubled and inverted surcharge	30
CUBA	
1899 10¢-on-10¢ special printing	32
CYPRUS	
1886 ½-piastre-on-½pi stamp	34

FANNING ISLAND
1911 1-penny provisional. 36

FIJI
1922-27 2-penny missing-value error 38

FRANCE
1849-50 1-franc Vervelle 40
1863-70 4-centime tete-beche pair. 42

GREAT BRITAIN
1865 9-penny plate 5 abnormal. 44
1867 10-penny error of watermark 47
1867-80 6-penny plate 10 abnormal. 49
1873-80 1-shilling abnormal. 52
1877 4-penny vermilion abnormal. 54

GUADELOUPE
1877 40-centime postage due 56

GUERNSEY
1979 unissued 11 pence 58

HAITI
1914 50-centime overprint. 60

HAWAII
1893 Provisional Government overprints 64

INDIA
1854 ½-anna printed on both sides. 67

ITALY
1852 Parma 15-centesimi tete-beche pair 69
1865 20-centesimo-on-15c inverted surcharge 71
1922 Offices in Ottoman Empire unissued stamp 73

LAGOS
1893 ½-penny-on-2d surcharge error. 75

MALTA
1919 10 shillings. 77

MARTINIQUE
1886-91 surcharges. 79

NATAL
1857 3-penny tete-beche pairs. 81

NAURU
1916-23 10-shilling indigo blue 83
NEW BRUNSWICK
1851 1 shilling.. 85
NEW ZEALAND
1906 1-penny claret...................................... 88
1963 1-shilling 9-penny missing color.................... 90
NEWFOUNDLAND
1860 1-shilling orange on laid paper..................... 91
PAPUA
1929 3-penny airmail with overprint omitted 94
PHILIPPINES
1944 1-peso Victory provisional 96
PORTUGUESE GUINEA
1881 misplaced cliche................................... 98
RHODESIA
1905 1-shilling imperforate between..................... 101
RUSSIA
1902-05 7-ruble inverted center 103
ST. HELENA
1868 1-shilling-on-6-penny missing surcharge............ 105
ST. LUCIA
1869 steamship local.................................... 108
ST. VINCENT
1861 6-penny yellow-green.............................. 110
1861 4-penny-on-1-shilling provisional 113
SERBIA
1872-79 1-para tete-beche pair......................... 115
SOUTH AUSTRALIA
1855 1-shilling violet.................................... 117
1903 "EIGNT" error..................................... 119
SOUTH GEORGIA
1928 2½-penny provisional.............................. 121
STRAITS SETTLEMENTS
1867 "2" on 1½-on½-anna.............................. 123
1899 5¢ missing surcharge 125

v

SWEDEN
1891 5-ore brown 127

SWITZERLAND
1935-38 10-centime+ inverted surcharge 129

TASMANIA
1853 4-penny Van Diemen's Land 131

TOBAGO
1880 6-penny bisect 133

TRANSVAAL
1869 1-shilling tete-beche pair 135

TURKEY
1868 Asia Minor Steamship locals 137

TURKS ISLANDS
1873 ½-penny-on-1-shilling 139

UNITED STATES
1860 2¢ Beckman carrier. 141
1898 8¢ Trans-Miss imperf-between 143
1908 coils 147
1916-17 30¢ perf 10. 151
1930 2¢ Von Steuben imperf. 153

URUGUAY
1867 60-centavo Diligencia. 155
1895 25-centesimo inverted center 158

VENEZUELA
1874 inverted frames. 161

INDEX 163

Introduction

In the heart of every stamp collector lies the dream that someday he will discover a philatelic gem — that unique stamp or cover heretofore unknown. Collectors spend hours peering through magnifying glasses, dipping stamps in watermark fluid, and examining stamps with ultraviolet lamps, hoping to find some tiny characteristic that makes their stamp different from all others.

Imagine the excitement of the collector who discovered a sheet of the British Solomon Islands' 2½-penny stamps with the perforations missing horizontally. Consider the joy experienced by the collector who, while examining a 2½-penny stamp through a magnifying glass, discovered that the fraction was missing its numerator.

The discovery of a ½-penny-on-2d surcharge error from Lagos surprised a stamp dealer who was evaluating an otherwise ordinary stamp collection.

These stories and more are told in the pages of *Philatelic Gems 4*. Like its predecessors *Philatelic Gems 2 and 3*, *Philatelic Gems 4* presents the seldom-told stories of many of philately's lesser-known rarities.

Few collectors are aware of the existence of an 1879 25-centime imperforate stamp from Bulgaria — the only one known to exist.

A collector in Austria discovered a copy of Great Britain's rare 1867-80 6-penny abnormal from plate 10. Another copy of this stamp was connected with the notorious Dr. Paul Singer, the stamp dealer who built a stamp empire out of a tiny stamp firm in Ireland. The empire collapsed and Singer disappeared, never to be heard from again. The 6d stamp, however, still exists.

Philatelic Gems 4 also tells of tragic endings to some of stampdom's great rarities. Several copies of two scarce Hawaiian provisionals disintegrated in a fire that resulted from the San Francisco earthquake in 1906. A local stamp from St. Lucia disappeared in the mail when it was being returned from a collector to its owner. The registered envelope carrying the rarity never arrived.

This book relates the fascinating stories behind many different types of gems. Four stamps from the Belgian Congo have been discovered with the centers of their designs inverted. Collectors know of only 10 copies of Haiti's 1914 50-centime stamp with both the "GL.O.Z." and "Poste Paye" overprints. Of these 10, two copies still are unaccounted for.

Only eight copies have been recorded of an unissued 1922 15-piaster-on-25-centesimo stamp of the Italian Offices in the Ottoman Empire. The Italian Post Office never released this stamp because it closed its offices in the empire. The stamp now ranks as one of the great airmail rarities of the world.

Two examples exist of the double-surcharge variety on the 1928 2½-penny provisional issued for South Georgia. Only 25 copies were produced of the 1886-91 5-centime-on-20c stamp overprinted for the French colony of Martinique.

A scarce tete-beche pair comes from the Italian state of Parma. Only seven copies have been recorded. Another tete-beche rarity comes from the South African province of Natal.

This book also presents the stories behind two rare bisects — one from the Canadian province of New Brunswick and the other from Tobago, an island in the British West Indies.

This fourth edition of *Philatelic Gems* once again introduces collectors to many rare, yet underrated stamps and covers. These seldom-told stories rekindle the fires in the hearts of stamp collectors, keeping the hope alive that someday they will discover one of the world's greatest rarities.

AUSTRALIA

A Fractured Fraction

VALUE: $3,500
The "1" is missing from the fraction on this used Australia 2½-penny definitive stamp from the 1915-24 series.

One of Australia's most interesting printing varieties is the 2½-penny stamp of the 1915-24 series with the figure "1" of the "½" fraction missing. This stamp is part of the third Kangaroo series of Australia. Stamp collectors can identify this series by the narrow crown and narrow A watermark.

Six colonies — New South Wales, Victoria, Queensland, South Australia, Western Australia and Tasmania — joined together in 1901 to form the Commonwealth of Australia. Twelve years passed before the Commonwealth issued its first stamps in 1913 featuring its familiar native animal, the kangaroo, and a map of Australia.

Although Australia issued a series of stamps bearing a portrait of King George V and also stamps showing the kookaburra, the kangaroo design continued in use for several years.

J.B. Cook, the government stamp printer, produced the Kangaroo stamps from 1913 until mid-1918, when T.S. Harrison, an Australian bank note printer, took over. The 2½d value was printed in dark blue, although several shades exist.

In 1921, a stamp collector discovered a most unusual variety on the 2½d. He found a stamp with the figure "1" of the fraction missing. Apparently, the printing electro became damaged, causing the omission of the "1." Later printings show the repaired fraction.

Mint examples of this variety are extremely scarce. The Scott catalog lists the rarity as number 46a and prices it at $10,000 mint and $3,500 used. At its November 19-23, 1985, auction in New York City, David Feldman SA sold a used copy of the missing "1" variety for $2,070, including a 15-percent buyer's premium.

A Taped Variety

VALUE: Indeterminable

What is often referred to as an inverted overprint actually is an inverted stamp on the Australian 6d Kangaroo Official of the 1932-33 series. The repair tags (right) are shown on the back of the stamp.

Penny-pinching efforts of Australia Post led to the creation of inverted overprints on its Official stamps.

In 1931, Australia Post stopped perforating its stamps with the letters "OS" for official use. (Collectors refer to these perforated initials as perfins.) These stamps were replaced by Official stamps overprinted "OS" in blue-black ink.

Oddly enough, the inverted overprints on these Official stamps come from repaired sheets. Prior to overprinting the sheets of regular issues for official use, Australia Post replaced defective stamps in the sheets with sound copies. The defective stamp was removed, and small strips of gummed paper from the selvage of the sheet were used to tape the new stamp in the sheet. The printer then applied the "OS" overprint.

Sometimes the replacement stamp was inserted upside down. The overprint was applied in the normal position and appears normal on all other stamps in the sheet. On the replacement stamp, however, the overprint appears inverted. (Actually, it is the stamp that is inverted.)

Inverted overprints appear on the ½-penny orange and 2d red King George V Officials of the 1932-33 series. These stamps are

VALUE: $3,500
An inverted overprint also appears on this ½-penny George V Official.

scarce. The Scott catalog lists the ½d (O6a) at $3,500 mint and $1,750 used. The 2d (O8) catalogs at $2,500 used.

In 1985, Australian stamp dealer J.G. Jude discovered the 6d chestnut Kangaroo Official of the same series with an inverted "OS" overprint. The stamp shows the repair tags on the back, indicating that the stamp replaced a defective copy in the sheet.

Jude sent the stamp to the Royal Philatelic Society's Expert Committee and received a certificate stating that the variety is genuine and that the stamp is "canceled to order from post office specimen pack." Jude says Australia Post applied a cancel to all stamps sold in its specimen packs, except the 10/-, £1 and £2 Kangaroos, which were overprinted "Specimen."

This is the only recorded copy of the 6d Official with an inverted overprint. The stamp has not received a listing in the Scott catalog.

AUSTRIA (Lombardy-Venetia)

A Taxing Situation

VALUE: $3,000
A used copy of the Lombardy-Venetia 4-kreuzer newspaper tax stamp.

One of the scarcest stamps of Lombardy-Venetia is a 4-kreuzer newspaper tax stamp used by the government to raise money. Lombardy-Venetia, also known as Austrian Italy, was a kingdom in northern Italy and formed part of the Austrian Empire. The kingdom issued stamps from 1850 to 1866. Lombardy was annexed to Sardinia in 1859. In 1866, Austria relinquished Venetia to Italy.

Austria issued its first newspaper tax stamp on January 3, 1853, to collect the fiscal fee on newspapers. This 2kr green stamp also was used in Lombardy-Venetia. Newspaper tax stamps differ from newspaper stamps in that the tax stamps cover a revenue fee; the newspaper stamps represent prepayment of postage.

On January 11, 1858, Lombardy-Venetia issued three newspaper tax stamps. These stamps differed from the Austrian newspaper tax stamps only in color. The Austrian stamps were 1kr blue, 2kr brown and 4kr brown. The Lombardy-Venetia stamps were 1kr black, 2kr red and 4kr red. Each featured the Austrian coat of arms.

On November 1, 1858, Austria revalued its currency. Lombardy-

Venetia used a currency based on silver. Austria used a paper currency. The fluctuations between the two currencies sometimes were considerable. The Lombardy-Venetia stamps were printed in different colors to prevent persons in Lombardy-Venetia from buying stamps in Austrian currency to take advantage of the exchange rate. Lombardy-Venetia stamps could be used in Austria, but Austrian stamps were not valid in Lombardy-Venetia. Although the Lombardy-Venetia newspaper tax stamps carried values in kreuzer, the public was charged soldis, the currency of Lombardy-Venetia. At the same time the currency was revalued, the newspaper tax fees were doubled from 1kr to 2kr for inland papers and from 2kr to 4kr for foreign papers.

The public protested so vehemently that on January 1, 1859, the government reduced the tax fees to the original rates. With the return to the original rates, there was no longer a need for the 4kr stamps. The stamps of this denomination saw little use. Most were destroyed. Today, these stamps are extremely scarce, particularly in mint condition. Many of the 4kr stamps that were used were removed from the newspapers by stamp collectors. The Scott catalog prices used copies of the 4kr red at $3,000. The much scarcer mint copies are listed at $40,000.

Reprints of these stamps exist. They were produced by the government in 1858, 1860 and 1863. According to the Scott catalog, the reprints are on smooth toned paper.

Siamese Overprints

VALUE: $1,210

This rarity was issued for three different countries — India, as a basic 2-anna stamp; Straits Settlements, as a 32¢-on-2a provisional; and Bangkok, with the "B" overprint.

Several rarities exist among the provisionals issued by the British Post Office in Bangkok from 1882 to 1885.

In 1881, Siam's King Chulalongkorn announced the organization of the kingdom's postal service. No stamps were available, so the British Post Office in Bangkok issued stamps for the new postal service. Great Britain exercised extraterritorial privileges in Bangkok from 1855 to 1885 as part of a treaty signed in 1855. The British overprinted a large black "B" on stamps of Straits Settlements portraying Queen Victoria.

As is typical of many overprinted and surcharged issues, varieties exist. The "B" is inverted on the 4¢ rose of the 1882 Bangkok issue and the 2¢ rose and 8¢ yellow orange of the 1882-83 series. The Scott catalog lists no price for the 4¢ invert of 1882. The 2¢ invert is priced at $12,500 mint and $3,000 used; the 8¢ invert catalogs at $4,500 used. Double overprints appear on the 2¢ rose, 6¢ violet and 10¢ slate of the 1882-83 series. Scott prices only the 2¢ rose double overprint — at $1,750 mint.

One of the scarcest stamps of Bangkok is the 30¢ claret of the first issue. It catalogs at $12,500 mint and $6,000 used. Two surcharged provisionals of Straits Settlements also were overprinted for use in Bangkok. In 1883, the overprint was applied to the 2¢-on-32¢ stamp. This provisional had been released by Straits Settlements earlier that year. In 1885, another Straits Settlements provisional, the 32¢-on-2-anna of 1867, was overprinted "B" for Bangkok. This stamp actually was released for three different countries. The basic 2-anna stamp was issued by India. In 1867, it was surcharged "32¢" for use in Straits Settlements. In 1885, the British overprinted it for use in Bangkok.

The 32¢-on-2a with the "B" overprint is extremely scarce. The Scott catalog lists it at $12,500 mint and $15,000 used. Christie's auctioned a mint copy at one of its Isleham collection sales March 11, 1987. The stamp realized $1,210, including the 10-percent buyer's premium. The "B" overprinted stamps were valid in Siam until Siam joined the Universal Postal Union in July 1885. At that time, Siam (now Thailand) began issuing its own stamps portraying Chulalongkorn.

A Topsy-Turvy Riverboat

VALUE: $22,185
Few examples have been recorded of this Congo Free State 1898 10-franc stamp with the center inverted.

Four major errors occurred during the printing of the bicolor pictorial series of stamps used in Congo Free State from 1894 to 1908 and Belgian Congo (now Zaire) from 1909 to 1923.

King Leopold II of Belgium became chief owner of the Congo Free State, which later became the Belgian Congo, by the Conference of Berlin of 1884-85. In 1886, Leopold's portrait appeared on the first stamps of the independent state.

But in 1894, a new series was introduced to publicize the Congo. It showed scenes indigenous to the African state. This series of pictorial stamps is known as the Mols because the engravings were taken from paintings by Mols and Van Engelen. Belgian Colonies collectors refer to all the 1894-1923 bicolored stamps (Scott 14-87) by the simpler name, Mols.

Waterlow and Sons Ltd. in England printed most of the Mols, including three of the inverts. Waterlow Brothers and Layton (also of London) printed one of them, the 10-franc inverted center of 1898. Both companies had to pass the sheets through the printing press twice — printing the black centers first and the frames (in various colors) in a second pass.

During the printing of the 10-centime blue and black stamp of the

1894-1901 series (Scott 18), two sheets of 50 were turned upside down during the second pass. This resulted in inverted centers (really inverted frames, although stamp collectors seldom refer to them as such) on those sheets. They then were line-perforated 14.

At least 65 of them eventually were obtained and sold by a London stamp dealer. Only one copy is known used, it being on a highly philatelic cover addressed to a dealer.

Since those 65 were dispersed at hugh premiums to stamp collectors, most of the stamps probably still exist. The stamp is still rare and desirable. John W. Kaufmann Inc. sold a copy in its December 6, 1985, sale of the David Melat collection for $660. Anoth-

VALUE: $8,250

Although 40 copies (in four sheetlets) of this Belgian Congo 1915 10-centime stamp were printed, this is one of only 10 now known. The inverts came from the same booklet.

er copy sold in the Christie's Zurich Brabant sale of May 13, 1987, for about $600.

In a subsequent printing of the same stamp, one sheet was likewise printed with inverted centers, but this stamp was line-perforated 15. Belgian Congo specialist Edgar A. Hirdler said the invert escaped notice until many of the stamps from the sheet had been routinely sold in the Congo. One knowledgeable Belgian recognized what it was, bought the remainder, and used them on controlled mail (mostly postcards) back to Belgium.

Hirdler said there are 14 known used. One of those was sold in the Brabant sale for about $1,200. One unused copy surfaced in 1979 and is in Hirdler's collection.

The Scott catalog lists the error at $1,500 mint and $1,900 used, but does not specify perforation. These prices should apply to the perf 14 and perf 15 varieties, respectively.

Much scarcer than the 10c inverts of the 1894-1901 series is a similar invert of the 10-franc stamp of 1898 showing a river steamer on the Congo River. The error — with its upside-down steamer — is even more striking than its earlier counterpart. The printer had repeated the mistake of the other printer by turning one sheet upside-down during the second pass through the press.

Few copies of the 1898 10fr invert have been recorded. Christie's auctioned one in its May 12-14, 1987, auction of the Isleham collection. It realized $22,185, including the 10-percent buyer's premium. The Scott catalog lists this error (30a) at $5,750.

Hirdler said that during World War I, after all the stocks of the 1910 issue (Scott 45-47, 49-50, 52, 54, 56-57, 59) in Belgium had fallen into German hands, the Mols were partially redesigned (5c, 10c and 25c) but printed in the 1910 frame colors to comply with Universal Postal Union regulations. The other values changed color. These were available for use in the Congo by late 1915 and are known as the series of 1915.

Several times thereafter, booklets were sold containing various numbers of sheetlets of 10 of the 5c, 10c, 15c and 25c. Unlike the other Mols, which were all printed in sheets of 50, Waterlow arranged 40 stamps in four groups of 10 on the printing plate, providing four booklet panes with margins all around after guillotining.

Hirdler said that during one printing of the 10c sheetlets, one sheet was turned upside down for the second pass. This created four booklet panes, each with 10 inverted centers. The normal pane is Scott 61d; the inverted center variety is unlisted.

Only one pane has been discovered. It has been broken up into a block of four and six singles, said Hirdler. The upper-left-corner margin single is pictured in DuFour's monumental work on Congo philately. A left margin single was auctioned by Cherrystone in its June 25-26, 1986, sale for $8,250.

Hirdler said that despite efforts by the Belgian Congo Specialists' Study Circle, no one has ever come forward with facts on what happened to the three other panes with inverted centers.

A Trial Run?

VALUE: $11,000
An example of Bermuda's controversial 1874 3-penny-on-1d provisional.

Bermuda's most controversial stamp is the 3-penny-on-1d surcharged provisional of 1874.

The Bermuda Post Office experienced a shortage of 3d stamps in 1874. In *The Postal History and Stamps of Bermuda*, M.H. Ludington said this shortage was a result of the "complex and unintelligible system of post office accounts." The Bermuda Post Office's accounts were so complicated that no one was aware there was a shortage of 3d stamps until it was too late. Supplies could not be obtained from the printer in England in time, so the post office was forced to issue provisional stamps.

The post office decided to convert a supply of its 1/- stamps to 3d. The stamps were individually handstamped by Sergeant Maddox of the Royal Engineers.

Ludington said it is apparent that the stamps were handstamped because the registration of the surcharges on adjoining stamps vary, and the impressions and inking are irregular. The surcharge consists of "THREE PENCE" in one line printed diagonally across the stamp from the lower left corner to the upper right.

Two types of the surcharge exist. The first is in roman capitals. The second is in fancy shaded italic capitals. A variety of the second type shows the "P" in "PENCE" with a fancy serif top like the "R" in "THREE." In 1875, the philatelic press reported the discovery of a 1d stamp surcharged with the "THREE PENCE" in the fancy italic type and with the plain "P." Surcharges also are found on the 2d stamp, but these are forgeries.

Major E.B. Evans, a Bermuda specialist in the 19th century, was the first to refer to the 1d and 2d surcharged stamps as essays. He said that the receiver general found a quarter of a sheet (60 stamps) of the 3d-on-1d stamps and gave it to a prominent collector, Sir Reginald Gray.

Major Evans said the stamps were from a trial sheet. The printer experimented on a sheet of the low-value 1d, rather than waste a sheet of the more costly 1/-.

The controversy over this stamp arose when used copies were discovered. Were these 1d stamps surcharged in error? Were they forgeries like the 2d?

In his Bermuda book, Ludington answered these questions. He referred to a record book of the receiver general. An entry for March 4, 1874, shows that 60 1d stamps were removed from the receiver general's stock. Ludington said this entry is bracketed in the cash column with the entry of March 9, 1874, showing the withdrawal of 4,500 1/- stamps for conversion into 3d stamps.

"Undoubtedly this entry refers to the quarter sheet, or pane of 60, of 1d stamps which were surcharged 'THREE PENCE,' although no mention is actually made as to the purpose of their withdrawal or destination of the stamps," Ludington stated. He went on to say, "There is no entry under 'Stamps Received,' either by itself or in combination with converted 1/- stamps, which allows for the inclusion of 60 extra surcharged stamps, so that it is evident that the 3d on 1d stamps were never returned to the receiver general's stock, but must have been those placed by him in his desk." Ludington concluded, therefore, that the 3d-on-1d surcharges are essays and were never intended to be issued.

Most of the used copies bear duplex cancellations of Hamilton or St. Georges. Ludington said these types of cancellations came into use June 1, 1879, so the surcharged stamps canceled with these markings are postdated by at least five years. A few of the 3d-on-1d stamps bear the bar cancellations of the correct period, but Ludington said these also could be postdated.

It is believed these essays were canceled and passed through the mails by favor and are philatelic in nature. Nevertheless, they are scarce and highly sought-after by collectors.

The Scott catalog lists the 3d-on-1d stamp with the notation that it "is stated to be an essay, but a few copies are known used." Scott prices the stamp at $15,000 mint, but lists no price for used copies. Christie's/Robson Lowe sold a mint example of this stamp at its March 11, 1987, Isleham collection auction. It realized $11,000, including a 10-percent buyer's premium.

Another Upside-Down Plane

VALUE: $1,250
Bolivia's 10-centavo airmail invert was desperately sought by Sanabria.

When Bolivia's 10-centavo National Aviation School invert was discovered, collectors predicted it would soon rank with the United States 1918 24¢ inverted Jenny. Although the error fell short of these expectations, it is one of Bolivia's scarcest stamps.

In December 1924, Bolivia issued its first set of airmail stamps to commemorate the founding of the National Aviation School. The airmail issues also were valid for ordinary postage. Soon after the set's release, rumors spread that a collector had discovered a sheet of 50 of the 10c with the center inverted.

During a visit to his native Venezuela, Nicolas Sanabria, airmail specialist and publisher of *The Standard Catalogue of Air Post Stamps*, made several attempts to locate the owner of the inverts. When the two finally met, Sanabria tried to convince the owner to sell the sheet, but he refused.

Sanabria returned to New York without the inverts, but he did not give up. He continued to hound the owner, trying to persuade him to dispose of the sheet. A few years later, the owner agreed to sell a few of the inverts to Sanabria, who broke the sheet into blocks and singles and offered them to collectors.

The National Aviation School set, Bolivia's first airmail issue, was printed by Perkins, Bacon & Company Ltd. in London. Each engraved stamp was printed in two colors. The frame of the 10c was printed in vermilion; the center, featuring the airplane, was printed in black. Two separate passes through the press were required. During the second pass, one sheet was turned upside down, resulting in the inverted centers.

Although Sanabria and the collectors who purchased the inverts predicted that this error one day would equal the U.S. inverted Jenny in value, this never happened. While the Jenny catalogs at $110,000 and has sold for much more than that, the Bolivian error is listed in Scott at $1,250 — an expensive stamp to be sure, but hardly on par with the Jenny. Harmers of London sold a copy of the Bolivian invert at its March 11-12, 1986, "Pegasus" auction. The stamp realized £632 (about U.S. $950).

Another invert in Bolivia's first airmail set — the 2 boliviano — was listed for several years in major stamp catalogs. Collectors now consider this a proof.

BRAZIL

The Pack Strip

VALUE: $275,000
The famous Pack strip of Brazil contains two 30-reis Bull's-Eyes stamps printed se-tenant with a 60r value.

A vertical strip of three of the Brazil Bull's-Eyes, consisting of two 30-reis stamps printed se-tenant with a 60r, is Brazil's number one rarity. This strip, known as the Pack strip, also ranks as one of the

17

top rarities of the world. The renowned collector Charles Lathrop Pack owned the strip, thus its name Pack strip.

The Bull's-Eyes were the world's second set of adhesive postage stamps, following behind Great Britain's Penny Black and 2d blue of 1840. The Bull's-Eyes made their debut on August 1, 1843. (The New York City Dispatch stamps were released in 1842 and the Zurich Numerals were issued in March 1843, but these have local status.) Collectors call Brazil's first issue Bull's-Eyes because they resemble the animal's eyes.

Although the Pack strip may appear to be a printing error, with the 60r printed in a strip of 30r stamps, it actually is a variety created during the separation of the panes.

The Brazilian State Mint produced the Bull's-Eyes stamps by recess engraving. The plate of 54 stamps consisted of 18 of each value of the Bull's-Eyes issue — 30r, 60r and 90r — in three panes. Each pane consisted of three horizontal rows of six stamps. The panes were separated by a horizontal dividing line.

Because the 30r and 60r were in greater demand than the 90r, the mint produced four additional plates — one plate of fifty-four 30r, a plate of sixty 30r, and two plates of sixty 60r.

The Pack strip came from sheets from the plate combining the three denominations. These sheets were not always cut into panes of just one denomination, as was intended. The horizontal dividing lines were ignored, resulting in pairs containing two different denominations. Such pairs are scarce.

The dividing line appears on the Pack strip between the 30r and 60r. The 60r is the bottom stamp. The Pack strip is believed to be unique. In addition to Pack, the strip was in the collections of Almedia, Dias and Admundsen.

Stanley Gibbons sold this item in a March 1963 sale for £8,250. When Robert A. Siegel Auction Galleries sold the Gordon N. John collection on May 25, 1986, the strip was part of the collection. It realized $275,000, including the 10-percent buyer's premium.

BRITISH SOLOMON ISLANDS

A Soldier's Prize

VALUE: $6,300
An example of the rare British Solomon Islands 2½-penny pair with the perforations omitted horizontally.

The British Solomon Islands contributes a stamp to the list of modern rarities, further proving that a stamp need not be 100 years old to be considered a philatelic gem.

Until 1936, when George VI became king of England, the stamps of the British Solomon Islands consisted of keyplate issues printed by De La Rue in England and portraying King George V.

There were only three exceptions. One was the Solomons' first issue, known as the Large Canoes. These stamps showed a war

19

canoe based on a design by Charles M. Woodford, the first resident commissioner of the British Solomon Islands. The stamps were lithographed by W.E. Smith Ltd. in Sydney, Australia.

The second exception was the set known as the Small Canoes. These stamps were similar in design to the first, but in a smaller format. They were printed by De La Rue in England.

The third exception was the 1935 Silver Jubilee and Coronation sets, which featured common designs used by other colonies.

The reign of King George VI marked the beginning of a new era in stamp designs for these Pacific islands. The British Solomon Islands issued its first pictorial series with the king's portrait in an inset and never returned to the monotonous keyplate issues.

The 1939-51 series consisted of 13 values depicting scenic views of the Solomons or subjects significant to the islands.

The Solomons entrusted two British printers with the production of these engraved stamps. De La Rue printed the 2-penny, 3d, 2/- and 2/6d stamps. Waterlow and Sons Ltd. printed the ½d, 1d, 1½d, 2½d, 4½d, 6d, 1/-, 5/- and 10/- values.

Few varieties occur on these stamps, but one major error exists. In his classic book on British Solomon Islands, published in 1956, Harold Gisburn said that only a year or so earlier, a collector had discovered a sheet of the 2½d stamp with the perforations missing horizontally. This stamp, printed by Waterlow, depicts a war canoe similar to the one shown on the first issue of the Solomons.

The collector discovered a full sheet of 60 of the errors. This sheet was broken up into pairs and blocks, most of which were sold in the United States. Gisburn illustrated a block of four, apparently from the center of the sheet.

The Bridger and Kay King George VI catalog carries a note that a partial sheet was found by a U.S. serviceman and taken back to the United States. The last American troops left the Solomons in 1950, so the error probably was discovered no later than that.

Harmers of London sold a copy at its October 15, 1985, auction for £3,410 (about $4,800). Phillips of London offered one pair in its November 26, 1987, auction. It realized £3,800 (about $6,300). The Scott catalog lists the errors at $10,000. This price is in italics, indicating infrequent sales or lack of pricing information.

Only One Copy

VALUE: Indeterminable
The only recorded copy of Bulgaria's 1879 25-centime imperf stamp.

Count Ferrari, the well-known French stamp collector, owned the only recorded copy of an eastern European rarity — an imperforate 25-centime stamp of Bulgaria.

Bulgaria issued its first postage stamps on June 1, 1879 — a set of five featuring the lion of Bulgaria. The Russian State Printing Works in St. Petersburg printed the stamps in two-color typography in sheets of 100 containing four panes of 25. The stamps were perforated 14½ by 15 — all except one 25c stamp, that is.

The wide-margined imperforate 25c first appeared in the June 1924 sales of the Ferrari collection in Paris. An American collector, Arthur Hind, bought the stamp.

Following Hind's death, the imperf 25c was sold in January 1935 in London to Theodore Champion. Jan Poulie later purchased the rarity. Today it is owned by Dragomir Zagorsky, a Bulgarian collector living in California.

The history of this stamp prior to its ownership by Ferrari and how it was produced are subject to speculation. Zagorsky assumes that the perforating machine was defective, leaving one of the end rows of the sheet imperforate. Were other examples of this imperf stamp destroyed?

The rarity is used, bearing a blue cancel of Tirnovo. The date of the cancel appears to be June 21 or November 21, 1881. It is difficult to determine if the month is "XI" or "VI."

The Scott catalog lists this stamp as number 3a but lists no price because of the infrequency of sales.

Bulgaria's Rose Lion

VALUE: $1,750 plus
Colonel Hans Lagerlof donated this Bulgarian cover — bearing the 5-stotinka error of color — to the Swedish Postal Museum in Stockholm.

    Although Bulgaria is not well-known for contributing to the list of the many philatelic gems of the world, at least one of its issues is a striking rarity. The stamp is an error of color — the 5-stotinka rose and pale rose of 1882. This value normally is printed in green and pale green.
    The 5st was one of a series of stamps issued by Bulgaria featuring the familiar Lion of Bulgaria coat of arms. This series, also known as the "Big Lion" stamps, was designed by Georgi Yakovlev Kirkov. All Bulgarian stamps, from its first issue in 1879 until 1889, were printed by two-color typography at the Russian

Stamp Printing Office in St. Petersburg, where Kirkov was director.

When the error of color first was discovered, collectors assumed the printers had made an understandable mistake — inserting a 5st cliche in a plate of the 10st, which normally was printed in rose and pale rose. The common coat-of-arms design must have created some confusion for the printers, and who could have blamed them if they had mistaken a cliche of one value for another value?

However, in *Kohl's Handbook*, editor Dr. Herbert Munk said this is not how the error occurred. Dr. Munk said a sheet of the error, from which four stamps were taken, was seen at the post office window. This proved that the error of color was created by using the incorrect ink rather than by inserting the 5st cliche in a plate of 10st.

This error is particularly scarce on cover. Colonel Hans Lagerlof, who compiled a magnificent collection of stamp rarities from a variety of countries, owned a cover bearing the 5st error of color. The cover was sent from Varna, Bulgaria, in 1888 to Hanover, Germany. In addition to the 5st error, it also carries the normal 5st green, a 10st rose, and 30st violet. Colonel Lagerlof donated this cover and many other rarities to the Swedish Postal Museum in Stockholm.

Other covers featuring this error include one canceled at "Varna Dtc. 25, 1887" bearing a single and an entire canceled at Sofia April 12, 1887, with the error used with several other values.

Count Ferrari, who compiled one of the world's most famous, and at the time, most complete collections, owned a copy of the error of color on piece. Scott catalog lists the stamp at $2,250 unused and $1,750 used.

An Occupational Hazard

VALUE: Indeterminable
One of five copies of the Bushire 5-kran stamp of 1915 with the British occupation overprint inverted.

Bushire's only claim to fame among stamp collectors is a series of overprinted stamps issued during the occupation of the Persian port in 1915. Some of these stamps are great rarities.

During World War I, Persia (now Iran) was the scene of fighting between British and German factions. On August 8, 1915, British forces occupied Bushire. The British confiscated stocks of Persian stamps and overprinted these issues "BUSHIRE/Under British/Occupation." in black.

The first overprints appeared on the stamps portraying Shah Ahmed. These supplies lasted a month, and the British began overprinting the Persian Coronation issue of 1915. The quantities of the Coronation stamps overprinted were small, accounting for the scarcity of these stamps today. The overprints catalog at $400 and up.

The scarcest of the normal issues is the 2-chahi stamp, of which only 18 exist. This stamp is extremely rare used. The Scott catalog prices it at $8,500 mint and $10,000 used.

Only 22 copies of the 5c exist. The stamp catalogs at $6,000 mint and $6,500 used. The 6c also is scarce, with only 29 recorded. It is listed in Scott at $5,500 mint and $6,000 used. Only 48 copies are recorded of the 3-toman stamp. It catalogs at $2,750 mint and $3,000 used.

But the gem of this overprinted Coronation issue is the 5-krans stamp with the overprint inverted. Only five copies of this error have been recorded. A used copy is in the Royal Collection in Buckingham Palace. The inverted overprint is listed in Scott without a price because so few sales of this error have been recorded.

Another rarity is the 1915 1c-on-5c surcharged stamp with the Bushire occupation overprint. This stamp catalogs at $12,000 mint. No used copies have been recorded.

Bushire's philatelic fame was short-lived. The use of Persian stamps resumed October 16, 1915.

Collectors are cautioned that fogeries of the British occupation stamps are common.

CAPE OF GOOD HOPE (Mafeking)

Boy Scout Stamps

VALUE: $16,100
The scarce 3-penny Baden-Powell stamp with the design reversed.

    Most people know of Robert Baden-Powell as the founder of the Boy Scouts. But Baden-Powell also was responsible for the release of a set of stamps from the Cape of Good Hope. While all of these stamps are valuable, one is extremely scarce.
    The British army sent Baden-Powell to the Cape Colony (Cape of Good Hope) during the Boer War. The Boer War was fought between Great Britain and the Boer republics of Transvaal and the Orange Free State between October 1899 and May 1902. It was one of Britain's costliest wars.
    During the siege of the town of Mafeking, Baden-Powell managed to hold back the Boers. To keep up morale in the town, he set up a local bicycle post to enable the soldiers to communicate with each other. A corps of cadets mounted on bicycles delivered the mail within Mafeking. Runners stealthily slipped through the Boer lines to deliver mail to post offices from which letters were forwarded to friends and relatives back home.

Baden-Powell ordered Mafeking's postmaster, J.V. Howat, to issue stamps for this local post. The stamps are printed on bluish paper, which gives them a blurred appearance.

The 1-penny stamp features a cyclist. The ribbon at the top reads, "SIEGE OF V.R. MAFEKING." At the bottom appears the inscription "LOCAL POST/ONE PENNY." The 3d stamp, which ex-

VALUE: $10,000
The Cape 1900 3-penny Mafeking issue measuring 21 millimeters wide.

ists in two types, portrays Baden Powell. The ribbon at the top reads, "MAFEKING 1900 SIEGE." The ribbon at the bottom is inscribed "POSTAGE THREEPENCE."

According to one story, the 3d stamp was to feature a portrait of Queen Victoria; however, when a search through the files in Mafeking produced no suitable picture of the queen, Baden-Powell's portrait was used instead.

One type of 3d is 18½ millimeters wide; the other is 21 millimeters wide. The 21-millimeter stamps are the scarcer of the two. The Scott catalog lists the 18½-millimeter type at $2,500 mint and $750 used; the 21-millimeter type at $10,000 mint and $1,650 used.

However, the 18½-millimeter stamps include the scarce varieties. Used copies of horizontal pairs imperforate between exist. The

Scott catalog lists them at $17,500. The stamp also is known with a double impression. This variety is listed at $15,000.

The scarcest of the varieties is a reversed design. The normal stamp shows Baden-Powell facing left. The reversed-design variety shows him facing right. The lettering also is backward. Postmaster Howat said the error occurred when the printer reversed the photographic plate. Only one sheet of 12 of this variety was produced.

Several years ago, the *London Philatelist* carried an article by J.R.F. Turner describing his discovery of a copy of the reversed-design variety. Turner said he searched for many years for a copy of the rarity. Messrs. Plumridge and Company, a London auction firm, sent him an auction lot of Mafeking issues for inspection. While examining the lot, he discovered a copy with Baden-Powell facing right. The stamp bore an "Apr. 30, 1900" postmark.

To avoid creating suspicion by submitting an unusually high bid for the lot, Turner instead picked a number of lots and instructed the auctioneer to buy them for him regardless of the price. Turner paid only £2 10/- for the Mafeking lot.

Today, the Scott catalog lists this stamp at $40,000 mint and $25,000 used. The stamp is listed under Cape of Good Hope as number 179c. David Feldman SA sold a copy of the error at its November 19-23, 1985, auction in New York City. It realized $16,100, including a 15-percent buyer's commission.

Double And Inverted

VALUE: $41,800
Only 10 copies exist of China's 2¢-on-3-candareen stamp of 1897 with the surcharge doubled and inverted.

One of China's great rarities is an error created during the surcharging of the 3¢ red revenue stamps. The stamp is the 2¢-on-3-candareen double surcharge with both surcharges inverted.

Although not as well known, the stamp is scarcer than its cousin, the 1897 $1-on-3c red revenue with the small surcharge. (The story of the small-surcharge variety appears in *Philatelic Gems 2*.) Thirty-five copies of the small-surcharge variety exist. Only 10 copies of the 2¢-on-3c error are known to have survived.

For many years, the Customs Office handled the mail in China, but in 1897, China established the National Post Office. At the same time, the units of currency were changed from candareen, mace and tael to dollars and cents.

The post office needed new stamps to reflect these changes. While the new stamps were being created, the post office ordered the surcharging of current stamps with new denominations in dollars and cents.

When supplies of regular postage stamps ran low, the post office ordered the surcharging of its 3¢ red revenue stamps.

The revenue stamps had been printed as a means of collecting a tax, but the public outcry against the tax was so great that the Customs Office decided against it. The Customs Office placed the revenue stamps in storage. When the post office became desperate for stamps, the revenues were called into service.

The Statistical Department in Shanghai surcharged some of the stamps itself; others were sent to a private printer commissioned by the Statistical Department. The private printer surcharged the stamps by creating a plate of 20 settings arranged in horizontal format (10 by 2). The printer then surcharged a sheet of 100 of the red revenues five times from top to bottom.

Unlike the private printer, the Statistical Department surcharged its stamps in panes of 25. Such was the case with the 2¢-on-3c.

The 2¢-on-3c stamp with the inverted surcharge is common. The Scott catalog lists it at $300 mint and $250 used. But only one pane of 25 was produced with the surcharge doubled and inverted. A recent realization attests to the rarity of the doubled and inverted surcharge variety. A copy of the stamp sold for $41,800, including the 10-percent buyer's premium, at the January 9, 1988, auction conducted by Michael Rogers, Inc. This was the first time in 17 years that a copy of this error had come onto the market, which explains the low Scott catalog price of $2,000. This also was the first public sale of the error.

The copy sold at the Rogers auction was once in the collection of Alfred Caspary. The collector who bought it from Caspary wishes to remain anonymous. The new owner of the stamp is from Switzerland and is a major collector of Chinese stamps.

Michael Rogers said this is one of the finest examples of the error known. The doubling is more pronounced on some of the stamps than on others. This copy shows obvious doubling.

CUBA

For Exposition Only

VALUE: $4,500
A vertical imprint pair of the 1899 10¢-on-10¢ type II special printing. This pair was in the Lilly collection.

Special printings created for the Paris Exposition of 1900 are among Cuba's great rarities. In accordance with the peace treaty of December 10, 1898, following the Spanish American War, Spain relinquished Cuba to the United States. The U.S. military ruled the island from January 1, 1899, to May 20, 1902, when Cuba assumed self-government.

During the period of U.S. administration, Cuba used U.S. stamps overprinted and surcharged for the island, until separate Cuban stamps were printed late in 1899.

In 1899, the committee for the Paris Exposition invited the U.S.

Post Office Department to exhibit examples of its current stamps. This exhibit was to include singles and blocks of four of all stamps issued by the U.S., including those used by U.S. possessions.

The Post Office Department ran into a problem, however, when it tried to show the stamps being used in Cuba. The Bureau of Engraving and Printing, which produced these stamps, had sent all supplies to Cuba.

In order to show a complete selection of stamps, the Post Office Department ordered a special printing of the Cuban surcharges especially for the exposition. Many copies of this special printing bear the handstamped "Special Surcharge" on the front or back.

One sheet each of the 1¢-on-1¢ yellow green, 2¢-on-2¢ carmine type III, 2½¢-on-2¢ red type III, 3¢-on-3¢ purple and 5¢-on-5¢ blue, as well as two sheets each of the surcharged postage dues and three sheets of the special delivery stamps, were printed.

The rarity of these special printings is the 10¢-on-10¢ brown type II. The normal surcharges for Cuba were on the U.S. 10¢ type I. For Cuba, type II was used only for the special printing, although it was used for other possessions. Type II can be distinguished from type I by the tips of the foliate ornaments below the white curved line below "TEN CENTS."

On type II, the tips of the ornaments break the curved line below the "E" of "TEN" and the "T" of "CENTS." On type I, the tips do not impinge on the curved line.

Most copies of the special printings were destroyed following the exposition. Few examples of the 10¢-on-10¢ exist. Scott catalog lists this rarity at $4,500 mint. The special printings were never used for postage.

Half And Half

VALUE: $8,500

The peculiar Cyprus 1886 surcharged ½-piastre stamp, type I, on Crown and CC watermarked paper.

An unusual surcharge occurs on the 1886 ½-piastre stamps of Cyprus. These stamps are surcharged "½ ½" even though the value tablet already reads "HALF PIASTRE."

Collectors unfamiliar with this issue could assume that this surcharge was an error. It was not. The postmaster of Cyprus ordered the stamps surcharged because of the possibility of color changelings in the basic stamps.

The ½pi stamps were printed in green, but sunlight or water easily changed the stamps' color to blue, the color of the 2pi stamp. To prevent the public from using the ½pi stamps as 2pi stamps, the postmaster ordered the stamps surcharged with the "½ ½" inscription.

In his book, *Cyprus*, Wilfrid T.F. Castle also offers the explanation that the peasants could understand the numerals easier than the English words on the value tablet. Since the ½pi stamp saw the most use, it became necessary to surcharge it.

Two types of surcharge exist. The two fractions on the smaller surcharge, known as type I, are 8 millimeters apart. The space is measured from fraction bar to fraction bar. The larger surcharge, type II, has a 6-millimeter space between the fraction bars.

The Cyprus Government Printing Office in Nicosia printed the 8-millimeter surcharge. Thomas De La Rue in London produced the 6-millimeter surcharge.

Most of the 1886 ½pi stamps appear on Crown and CA watermarked paper. However, a very few copies exist on Crown and CC watermarked paper. These Crown and CC copies rank among the great rarities of Cyprus. Extremely scarce are Crown and CC copies with the type II surcharge.

Castle quotes a 1936 address by the renowned Cyprus collector A.L. Pemberton concerning these rarities. Referring to the ½pi on Crown and CC paper with the type II surcharge, Pemberton said, "The status of this stamp is extremely doubtful. Very few copies are known, and these are all unused, so that at best it can be considered a proof or unissued variety. I have seen only three specimens, and found that the measurements were not exactly the same as those on the stamps watermarked Crown CA, while the impression of the surcharge was also different."

Pemberton questioned why 17 years had lapsed before the type II rarities were reported. The type I Crown and CC watermarked stamps were first reported in *The Philatelic Journal of Great Britain* in April 1893, only seven years after the stamp was first issued.

Although collectors today continue to speculate that the type II rarities are proofs, these stamps are considered among the great rarities of Cyprus. The Scott catalog prices the type I Crown and CC stamps at $8,500 mint and $750 used. The type II Crown and CC stamps, which still are recorded only in mint condition, are priced at $8,500.

A copy of the type I Crown and CC stamp was offered at the September 14, 1988, auction by Colonial Stamp Company. It realized $1,100, including the 10-percent buyer's premium.

The Obscure Handstamp

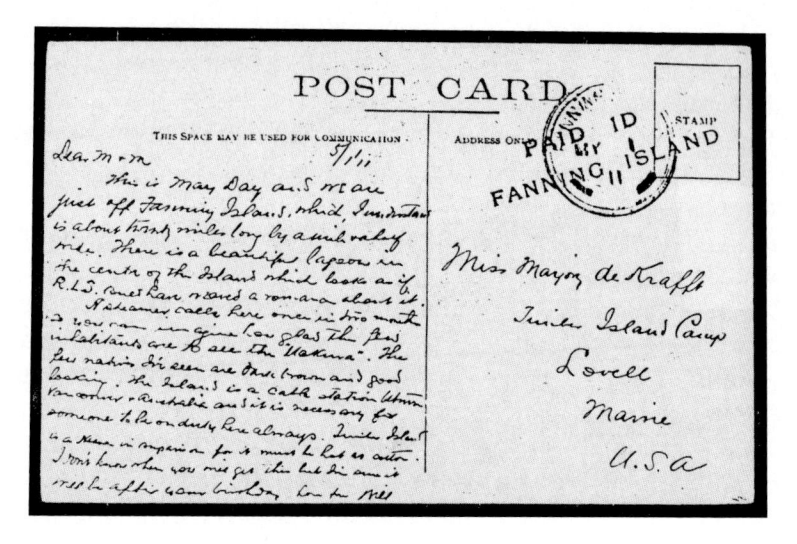

VALUE: Indeterminable

The "PAID 1D/FANNING ISLAND" provisional appears on this postcard addressed to Timber Island Camp, Lovell, Maine. The card, postmarked May 1, 1911, is the earliest known usage of the Fanning provisional.

A scarce provisional exists from a little-known island in the Pacific. Fanning Island is one of the Line Islands located 150 miles northwest of Christmas Island and 1,500 miles from Tarawa, the capital of Gilbert Islands, which the Line Islands belong. Captain Edmund Fanning of the United States brig *Betsy* discovered Fanning Island in 1798.

In 1902, The New Zealand Post Office opened a postal agency on Fanning. David Cuthbert was appointed the first postmaster. The post office opened the agency primarily to serve the staff of the Pacific Cable Board. The transpacific telegraph cable was laid in 1902, and a relay station was opened on Fanning that year.

Fanning never issued its own stamps. It used those issued by Great Britain, New Zealand and, later, Gilbert and Ellice Islands.

However, a scarce provisional resulted from a shortage in stamps on the island.

Steamers collected the mail from Fanning about once a month. In early 1911, the new postal agent, C.L. Hertzlet, anticipated a shortage of 1-penny stamps. He cabled the New Zealand Post Office and requested permission to surcharge other values of New Zealand stamps. The post office denied the request. But Hertzlet was given permission to produce a handstamped provisional. This provisional, struck in blue, reads, "PAID 1D/FANNING ISLAND."

The marking was used for only a short period, thus accounting for its scarcity. In *Philatelic Handbook of the Gilbert and Ellice Islands*, author D.H. Vernon says that only 50 1d stamps were available for the 100 or so letters mailed at that time from Fanning. The other letters apparently received the provisional.

Residents on Fanning, other than natives, numbered only about 35 in 1911. The natives seldom wrote letters, so the amount of mail leaving the island was small. Michel Forand, a Canadian collector, says that only 10 covers or postcards bearing this provisional have been recorded. Forand owns two of these — a cover and a postcard. Forand says that the postcard, which is postmarked May 1, 1911, is the earliest known date of usage.

The Stray-Paper Case

VALUE: $1,380

The only example of Fiji's 1922-27 2-penny missing-value error is the center stamp in this block of nine. An extraneous piece of paper caused the error. It also affects the stamps to the left and directly below the missing-value error and the stamp in the bottom left-hand corner.

    A stray piece of paper resulted in a missing-value error on a Fijian stamp. Only one example of this error has been recorded. It is contained in a block of nine stamps.
    The stamp is the 2 pence of the 1922-27 George V keyplate definitives. These single-color gray stamps were printed in two pro-

cesses. The portrait and most of the framework were printed in the first pass through the press. During the second pass, the country name and face value were applied.

The error occurred when a nearly square piece of paper lodged itself between the stamp sheet and the plate during the printing process. The paper blocked out not only the value on the center stamp of the block but also affected surrounding stamps.

This is the only error of this type to occur on any of the keyplate issues. Keyplate issues were used by many of the British colonies from the time of Queen Victoria through the early part of the reign of Queen Elizabeth II.

The value is completely missing on the center stamp. The stamp to the left of this shows only part of the "d" in "2d." The stamp in the bottom left-hand corner is missing the second "I" of "FIJI" and the ornament to the right. The stamp below the one with the value missing features only the bottom half of "FIJI" and the ornaments in the top tablet. All other stamps in the block are normal.

The block was first discovered in the 1930s. Temple Bar Auction sold the block at its September 23, 1980, sale for £1,350 and again at its March 1, 1985, auction for £2,500.

David Melat, an oil magnate from western Pennsylvania who put together one of the most extensive British Commonwealth stamp collections ever formed, acquired the block.

David Feldman SA sold this item when it dispersed of the Melat collection at its November 19-23, 1985, auction in New York City. Muscott's of Godalming paid $1,380, including a 15-percent buyer's commission, to buy the block at the auction.

The Stanley Gibbons catalog lists the error but gives no price. The Scott catalog does not list this item.

FRANCE

The Vervelle Variety

VALUE: $18,000
This copy of the 1-franc Vervelle was owned by Alfred Caspary.

Anatole Hulot, an eccentric 19th-century French printer, created France's greatest stamp rarities. Among these are the famous 1-franc Vervelle stamps of the 1849-50 series.

Hulot produced the extremely scarce tete-beche pairs of the Ceres series. Although his mysterious printing techniques have never been revealed, many collectors are convinced that he purposely reversed the cliches in the printing plates of this series to create tete-beche pairs. Tete-beche pairs have one stamp upside down in relation to the other.

France's tete-beche pairs were discussed in *Philatelic Gems 1*.

When Hulot died, his nephew, M.A. Huet, inherited an old trunk that belonged to the printer. Huet sold the trunk to a Parisian stamp dealer named Ernest Vervelle.

When Vervelle opened the trunk, he discovered sheets of early French stamps. Included among these treasures was one un-gummed sheet of 1-franc Ceres stamps in a pale shade of vermilion. This shade is distinctively different from the normal dull orange red used for the 1fr and also distinguishable from the vermilion on yellowish paper known as Scott 8a.

Collectors refer to the pale vermilion stamps as the Vervelle issue, in honor of the Parisian stamp dealer who first purchased

40

them. The variety is listed as Scott 8c.

Upon closer inspection of the sheet, Vervelle made an even greater discovery. The sheet contained one tete-beche pair — the mark of Hulot. This is the only example of this tete-beche pair. The tete-beche variety was removed from the sheet as a block of four.

Count Ferrari, the famous French collector, owned the block of four. Arthur Hind bought the block at the Ferrari auction. When Hind's collection was sold in 1933, the block realized about $6,000.

Alfred Caspary, another famous collector, owned a sheet-margin copy of the Vervelle. The Scott catalog prices the 1fr Vervelle at $18,000. The tete-beche pair is not listed.

FRANCE

The Auditor's Discovery

VALUE: Indeterminable
This block of nine of the French 4-centime stamp showing the tete-beche variety (center stamp) was in the Ferrari collection. The stamp is part of the 1863-70 Napoleon series.

Auditors are credited with discovering copies of France's rare 1863-70 4-centime tete-beche stamps in a drawer at Stanley Gibbons Ltd. in London.

Following the victory of the armies of Napoleon III in Italy in 1861, the emperor ordered that new stamps and coins be issued showing his portrait. The portrait showed Napoleon wearing a laurel wreath on his head to denote victory. The French Post Office had a large supply of stamps from the previous issue on hand and did not begin to release the new stamps until 1863. Post offices probably would not be so conservative today.

During the printing of the 4c, the printer replaced a defective cliche. In doing so, he accidentally inserted the new cliche upside down, creating the tete-beche variety. In a tete-beche pair, one stamp is inverted — or upside down — in relation to the others.

The late Charles J. Phillips, who once owned the Gibbons' company, told the story of the discovery of copies of the 4c tete-beche variety. Phillips recalled that in 1897 auditors from Ventom, Bull and Cooper arrived at Gibbons to conduct their audit of the stamp firm's inventory. Gibbons kept its wholesale stamp stock in 300 large drawers that towered up to the ceiling in the stockroom.

One of the auditors, eager to do a thorough check of the stock, climbed a ladder and removed one of the drawers from the top row. The drawer was so high that no one had bothered to look inside it for years. When the contents were revealed, the auditor found full sheets and partial sheets of French stamps. Among these were five full sheets of the 4c Napoleon with a tete-beche pair in the top row of each sheet.

A further search through some old envelopes revealed another tete-beche pair in a block of 16 stamps.

Phillips said Stanley Gibbons, the founder of the firm, probably had imported the stamps at face value.

The French count, Phillippe Ferrari, one of the world's most famous stamp collectors, owned an entire sheet of 150 with the 4c tete-beche pair. He also owned a block of nine showing the variety. These were sold when the Ferrari collection was auctioned by France in 1924. Today, the Scott catalog lists the tete-beche pair at $10,000 mint and $7,500 used.

The 4c tete-beche pair was not the only rarity to occur during the printing of the 1863-70 Napoleon series. The famous 5-franc with the value missing is also part of this series. This error was discussed in *Philatelic Gems 2*.

A Gift From the King

VALUE: $17,000

The rare Great Britain 9-penny plate 5 abnormal of 1865 was created as a memento to celebrate the Uniform Penny Postage Jubilee in 1890. The stamps were perforated, mounted in special albums and given to members of the British stamp committee.

One of Great Britain's most interesting rarities was created as a memento for members of the British Post Office's stamp committee. In 1865, the British Post Office issued a new series of stamps. These stamps feature a portrait of Queen Victoria with white check letters in the four corners. The plate number appears in the lower left and right corners above the check letters.

The series consists of 3-penny, 6d, 9d, 10d and 1/- values, all printed on heraldic emblems watermarked paper.

The 9d straw was the last value to be introduced in this series. Only plate 4 was used for producing this stamp. However, a proof, or imprimatur, sheet was produced for the 9d from plate 5. No 9d stamps from plate 5 were actually issued.

Then, in 1890, the Board of Inland Revenue decided to prepare mementos for members of the stamp committee to celebrate the Uniform Penny Postage Jubilee. Thirty-six examples of the 1865 9d straw were taken from the plate 5 imprimatur sheet on file in the postal archives at Somerset House to produce souvenirs for the stamp committee members. These stamps were line perforated 14 and mounted in an album entitled *Before and After the Stamp Committee.* Noted philatelic writer L.N. Williams, who has written extensively on the subject of the British abnormals, says that 12 of the 36 examples were returned to Somerset House and stuck back on the imprimatur sheet. At least 12 of the perforated stamps were used in the albums.

The British abnormals are surface-printed stamps produced during the reign of Queen Victoria. For each plate, it was customary for six proof sheets to be printed. One of these sheets (known as an imprimatur) went into the archives at Somerset House. The others sometimes were perforated and issued, although they frequently differed from the regularly issued stamps in color, paper, watermark or perforation.

Such was the case with the 9d from plate 5. Only, this time no stamps exist from the other five sheets. It is presumed that these sheets were destroyed prior to 1890. For this reason, the stamps for the presentation albums were taken from the imprimatur sheet rather than from one of the other five sheets.

No used copies of the 9d abnormal are known. However, in the *History of the Adhesive Stamps of the British Isles* by Hastings E. Wright and A.B. Creeke Jr., the authors record a used copy.

As with all stamps of the British Commonwealth, examples of the stamps from the presentation albums were placed in the Royal Collection at Buckingham Palace.

In 1916, King George V asked that the stamp bearing the check letters "K-L" be mounted on a card to be sold to benefit the National Philatelic War Funds. Sir Edward Denny Bacon, who was then curator of the collection, complied with the request.

The card is signed by Sir Edward and the king. It bears the inscription, "This 9d Plate 5 Gt. Britain stamp was taken from my collection and given to the National Philatelic War Funds Auction in September 1915. George R.I."

At the March 13, 1916, auction, Stanley Gibbons Ltd. purchased the card for £280 and immediately returned it for resale. Frank

Godden, another stamp dealer, bought it for £245. Most recently, this item was auctioned by Corinphila in Zurich, Switzerland, March 10-15, 1980. On November 15, 1979, Stanley Gibbons Ltd. sold a copy of the 9d plate 5 lettered "K-J."

An example lettered "L-K" was auctioned by Phillips in Great Britain on June 5, 1980. Gibbons sold an "N-K" example as part of the John O. Griffiths surface-printed collection on February 12, 1981. This copy again was sold June 30, 1986, by Colonial Stamp Company for $14,850, including a 10-percent buyer's premium.

The most recent sale of a 9d abnormal was by Christie's on March 11. This example, part of the Isleham collection, realized $10,450, including a 10-percent buyer's premium.

The Scott catalog lists this stamp at $17,000.

A copy lettered "N-J" is in the Reginald M. Phillips collection in the British National Postal Museum in London.

The Wrong Paper

VALUE: $21,450

This 1867 10 pence on heraldic-emblems watermarked paper is an error of watermark, not an abnormal.

A printer's error resulted in Britain's scarce 1867 10-penny red-brown stamp on paper with a heraldic-emblems watermark. The British Post Office introduced the 10d value in 1867 to pay postage to India, Mauritius and Australia. The stamp was part of the surface-printed, or typographed, series that made its debut in 1865.

These stamps featured a portrait of Queen Victoria facing left. The frame featured white check letters in each corner, for security purposes. The plate number appears twice on each stamp. On the 10d, the plate number 1 appears in a circle above the check letters in the bottom left and right corners.

The 10d stamp, along with other values in the 1867-80 series, was to be printed on spray-of-roses watermarked paper. However, the printer, Thomas De La Rue in London, failed to follow instructions. The company printed a few of the stamps on the heraldic-emblems watermarked paper used for the 1865 set.

Collectors sometimes refer to the 10d on heraldic-emblem paper

47

as an abnormal. For each plate of the British surface-printed stamps, it was customary for six proof sheets to be printed. One of these sheets (known as an imprimatur) went into the archives of the British Post Office. The others sometimes were perforated and issued, although they frequently differed from the regularly issued stamps in color, paper, watermark or perforation. These stamps are known as abnormals.

The 10d on heraldic-emblems watermarked paper, however, is not an example of an abnormal. It is an error. The printer simply used the wrong paper.

This rarity has a cousin — the 1867-80 10d red-brown from plate 2 — that is classified as an abnormal. Plate 2 was never sent to press. The story of this abnormal appears in *Philatelic Gems 3*.

De La Rue experienced problems in the positioning of the electrotypes on plate 1, causing perforating difficulties. A new plate was ordered, but before it could be sent to press, the postal rates were changed, leaving little demand for the 10d value.

Only 10 copies of the 10d plate 1 on heraldic-emblems watermarked paper have been recorded. Of these, seven bear the postmark of the British Post Office in Constantinople. The postmark consists of a large "C" in bars. A copy of the 10d error of watermark, lettered "RJ," is in the Reginald M. Phillips collection in the National Postal Museum in London.

Christie's of New York auctioned a copy lettered "LJ" in its March 11, 1987, sale of the Isleham collection. According to the auction catalog, I.J. Bernstein discovered this stamp in 1920. It was once in the Worthington and Calvert collections. The stamp realized $21,450, including a 10-percent buyer's premium, at the March 11 auction. The Scott catalog lists this stamp as number 47 and prices it at $18,500 used.

GREAT BRITAIN

Never Put To Press

VALUE: $18,700
A collector in Austria discovered this copy of Great Britain's rare 1867-80 6-penny abnormal from plate 10.

Fewer than a dozen copies of Great Britain's 1867-80 6-penny deep violet abnormal have been recorded. This is one of the scarcest of the abnormals. The abnormals are British surface-printed stamps produced during the reign of Queen Victoria. For each plate, it was customary for six proof sheets to be printed. One of these sheets (known as the imprimatur sheet) went into the archives of the British Post Office. The others sometimes were perforated and issued, although they usually differ from the regularly issued stamps in color, paper, watermark or perforation.

The rare 6d comes from plate 10. This plate, although registered April 1, 1869, was never put to press. The imprimatur sheet was the only sheet ordered for plate 10; however, a few sheets apparently were run off at the same time. These later were perforated and issued along with the regular stamps.

Christie's auctioned a copy of the 6d abnormal in its March 11, 1987, Isleham sale in New York City. The stamp realized $18,700, including the 10-percent buyer's premium, exceeding the Scott catalog value of $15,000. The auction catalog states that only six copies of the stamp are recorded. However, noted British writer L.N. Williams has recorded 10 examples.

The example sold by Christie's has a particularly interesting history. In 1935, a collector in Hollywood, California, found a copy of the abnormal bearing the letters H-Q in the lower corner squares. This discovery was much publicized, particularly when the stamp realized £155 in a London auction.

According to Williams, a collector in Austria heard of the discovery. The hope of making a discovery of his own lies in every collector's heart, and the Austrian was no exception. He immediately went to his collection to check his copy of the 6d stamp. Sure enough, the stamp bore the plate number 10 in the circles above the lower letters. His copy was lettered O-K and canceled "SE/13."

The Austrian sold it in a Harmers auction on June 23, 1936, for £190. J. de R. Phillp bought the stamp. Robson Lowe sold the O-K example in his November 4, 1959, sale for £550.

Another copy of the 6d abnormal with an interesting history is the stamp lettered G-B and canceled "545." Harmers of London sold this stamp on January 16, 1956, for £270.

Williams said the stamp was listed in the April 4, 1959, sale conducted by Shanahan, the Irish auction firm run by the notorious Dr. Paul Singer. The rise of Singer, his eventual downfall and his escapades in between are detailed in Seamus Brady's book *Doctor of Millions*. Singer built a stamp empire out of a tiny stamp firm in Dun Laoghaire, Ireland. He even pursuaded one of the world's most prominent collectors, the late Maurice Burrus, to consign his fabulous collection to the auction firm.

Following a mysterious burglary, Singer's stamp empire collapsed. Several lawsuits were filed against him. The court proceedings lasted four years. Singer disappeared and has never been heard of again in the stamp world.

The G-B example of the 6d abnormal was in the Burrus collection. When Robson Lowe sold part of the collection on October 30, 1963, the stamp realized £1,000.

The Beaumont copy of the abnormal set a record price for this stamp when it was sold by Phillips in London on April 12, 1984. Williams said that prior to World War II, this stamp, lettered K-I, was taken from Austria to South America and sold to a dealer in New

York. H.M. Beaumont bought it at a Harmers sale in London in 1949. When Robson Lowe sold the Beaumont collection on December 7, 1965, the stamp realized £300.

This example realized a record-breaking £12,650, including the 10-percent buyer's premium, at the Phillips auction in 1984.

Other copies of this abnormal recorded by Williams are lettered C-A, D-A, E-H, M-L, P-B and Q-K.

Only Five Known

VALUE: $15,000
This copy of the scarce British 1873-80 1/- abnormal from plate 14 is in the Phillips collection at the National Postal Museum in London, England.

One of the scarcest of the British abnormals is the 1873-80 1/- green printed from plate 14. Only five copies have been recorded. The abnormals are British surface-printed stamps produced during the reign of Queen Victoria. For each plate, the printer customarily printed six proof sheets. One of these sheets (known as an imprimatur) went into the archives of the British Post Office. The other five sheets sometimes were perforated and issued, although they frequently differed from the regularly issued stamps in color, paper, watermark or perforation.

Great Britain's 1/- green was printed on spray of roses watermarked paper and issued in September 1873. Plates 8 to 13 were used for this issue. Registration sheets of stamps from plate 14 also were perforated and put into use.

The abnormals are the stamps from these registration sheets. The plate number appears in two circles on both sides of the portrait of Queen Victoria.

The first copy of the 1/- green abnormal was recorded in 1915. Only four additional copies have been found since that time.

In 1976, Robson Lowe Ltd. offered a previously unrecorded example at auction. This stamp, lettered F-E in the lower corners, was badly trimmed at left and cut into at right. The stamp failed to find a buyer at the Robson Lowe sale.

L.N. Williams, the noted authority on British abnormals, describes the other four copies as follows:

A 1/- stamp lettered A-I was auctioned by H.R. Harmer on May 23, 1951. A copy lettered A-L and postmarked "Greenock" March 14, 1876, is in the Royal Collection at Buckingham Palace.

Another stamp, lettered C-L, is in the Reginald M. Phillips collection at the National Postal Museum in London. Williams says this stamp came from the collection of H.C.V. Adams, who co-authored *The Postage Stamps of Great Britain* with K.M. Beaumont.

The fourth copy of the abnormal, lettered D-H, is used on piece. It has the perforations at right and part of the wing margin at right cut away. The perfs at the top are trimmed. This stamp was auctioned by Stanley Gibbons on November 27, 1970. It realized £1,500.

The Scott catalog lists this as a variety of number 64. The stamp is priced at $15,000 used, the only condition in which it exists.

The Red Queen

VALUE: $20,350

The whereabouts of only five examples of Great Britain's 1877 4-penny vermilion abnormal are known today.

Although eight copies of Great Britain's 1877 4-penny abnormal have been recorded, the whereabouts of only five are known today. Two of these are in museums, with little chance of coming on the stamp market again.

The abnormals are from registration sheets of British surface-printed stamps issued during the reign of Queen Victoria. For each plate, the printer customarily printed six registration sheets. One of these sheets (known as the imprimatur) went into the archives of the British Post Office. The other five sheets sometimes were perforated and issued along with the regular issues. The abnormals frequently differed from the regularly issued stamps in color, paper, watermark or perforation.

Great Britain issued its 4d vermilion stamp on March 1, 1876. The stamp portrayed Queen Victoria facing left. It was printed on large-garter watermarked paper. Check letters appear in the four corners of the stamp for security purposes. The letters are printed in the same color as the stamp, against a white background. The plate number appears in circles on both sides of "POSTAGE." The printer used plate 15 for the 1876 issue.

Early in 1877, the British Post Office released stamps from the registration sheets printed from plate 16. These were printed in vermilion on the same watermarked paper as the earlier 4d vermilion stamps. Once again, the plate number appears in circles on both sides of "POSTAGE."

Shortly thereafter, the post office ordered the color of the 4d stamps changed to olive green. Postal officials had received complaints that the 4d vermilion stamps were easily mistaken for the 8d orange of the same issue.

As previously stated, two examples of the 4d abnormal are owned by museums. One copy, lettered E-J in the lower corners, is in the Royal Collection at Buckingham Palace in London. The other copy, lettered P-L, is in the National Postal Museum in London as part of the Reginald M. Philips collection.

L.N. Williams, the foremost authority on the British abnormals, records three other examples.

One stamp, lettered E-G, has a wing margin at left. Williams says the stamp bears an indistinct postmark, which is possibly "936." Stanley Gibbons Ltd. sold this copy on November 27, 1970, at its fourth auction of the "Maximus" collection. It realized £2,500.

A stamp lettered R-A and postmarked "383" was sold by Harmer, Rooke and Company at its November 28, 1956, auction.

The most recent sale of the 4d abnormal was by Christie's in New York City. The stamp, lettered I-H and postmarked "561," realized $20,350, including a 10-percent buyer's premium, at the Christie's March 11, 1987, Isleham sale. The Scott catalog lists the 4d abnormal as number 69 and prices it at $15,000.

GUADELOUPE

Dues Are First

VALUE: $26,000
Only 24 copies have been recorded of Guadeloupe's 1877 40-centime postage due stamp on bluish paper.

Guadeloupe's 40-centime postage due stamp of 1877 is one of the scarcest issues of the French colonies. Only 24 copies of this stamp have been recorded.

Guadeloupe lies in the West Indies between Montserrat and Dominica. In 1876, postal authorities of Guadeloupe, at that time a French colony, divided the colony into three postal areas. The authorities also restructured the postal rates so that it cost more to send a letter to a different postal area than to send it to an address within the same postal area. At the same time, mailboxes were placed outside the post offices for use when the post offices were closed. Several individuals took advantage of these. They placed letters in the boxes without affixing stamps.

To bring a halt to this practice, the postal authorities issued imperforate 25c and 40c postage due stamps. Both stamps feature the same ornamental frames. The central design shows either "25" or "40" with "centimes/a/percevoir." The English translation for "a percevoir" is "to collect." No country name appears on the stamps. The 25c was printed in black on white. The 40c was printed on bluish paper. The 40c was poorly printed and difficult to read because of the bluish paper. It was replaced in 1878 by a new 40c postage due stamp printed in black on white paper.

The 1878 stamp differs from the first issue in that it features much larger numerals and "centimes" is abbreviated "c." The frame is the same. In the November 1982 issue of the *American Philatelist*, the journal of the American Philatelic Society, Robert G. Stone, who specializes in French colonies, said that all 24 recorded copies of the 40c on bluish paper are postmarked or were used between March 1877 and March 1878. Six covers exist bearing this rarity. One cover, dated May 31, 1877, is franked by a pair. Five of the six are from the Lamentin Post Office.

Stone said that "from a 'plating' analysis of the known stamps (frames are the same as on the 25c, of which a sheet of 20 is available), Rifaux concluded that only three sheets of the blue were actually used." The Scott catalog lists the 40c on bluish paper as number J2 and prices the stamp at $26,000.

These postage dues interest stamp collectors for another reason: They were the first adhesive stamps issued by Guadeloupe. The colony's first regular issue wasn't released until 1884.

A Child's Discovery

VALUE: $30,000

Only one copy of the unissued 11-penny Guernsey Post Office Anniversary stamp has been discovered.

A child, working on his stamp collection, snipped a stamp off a first-day cover and soaked it off the extraneous paper. What the child did not realize was that the stamp was an unissued stamp that had escaped destruction. He had soaked one of Guernsey's scarcest stamps.

Guernsey, a group of islands in the English Channel, achieved postal independence from Great Britain in 1969, along with its fellow Channel island, Jersey.

In 1979, the Guernsey Post Office ordered a set of stamps to mark its 10th anniversary. The set was to consist of four values to cover the bailiwick rate of 6 pence, the British Isles rate of 8p, the Zone B airmail rate of 11p and the Zone C airmail rate of 13p.

Although Guernsey's post office is independent of the British Post Office, its postal rates are set by Great Britain. Six weeks before the Anniversary issue was to be released, the British Post Office increased its airmail rates. Rates for Zone B increased to 13p and Zone C to 15p.

The 11p value in the Anniversary set was rendered obsolete. It covered no specific postal rate. At the same time, there was a need for a 15p stamp to cover the new Zone C airmail rate.

The Anniversary stamps, including the 11p, had already been

58

printed by Courvoisier of Switzerland. The Guernsey Post Office ordered the sheets of 11p stamps destroyed. Courvoisier was asked to produce a 15p stamp using the design originally intended for the 11p. This design showed the Guernsey Post Office philatelic department.

One copy of the 11p escaped the shredder. The stamp the young collector soaked off the first-day cover was this copy of the

This 15-penny Guernsey Post Office stamp was issued with the design originally intended for the 11 pence.

unissued 11p stamp. The stamp bears the word "Issue," from the "First Day of Issue" cancel, in the top left-hand corner

The stamp has had several owners. In 1978, the Channel Islands Stamp Company acquired the rarity. Most recently, Alan Benjamin, a British dealer who specializes in errors and varieties, sold the unissued stamp for nearly $30,000.

Stanley Gibbons mentions the existence of the 11p in its British Commonwealth catalog, noting that the stamp was not issued for postal use. It is unlisted and unpriced.

It is unlikely that just one stamp from the sheet of 50 was rescued, but only one example has been discovered. How this stamp escaped destruction and wound up being used on a first-day cover is subject to speculation. Do others exist?

The Missing Copies

VALUE: $3,000

Only 10 copies have been recorded of Haiti's 1914 50-centime stamp bearing both the "GL.O.Z." and the "Poste Paye" overprints. Two of the 10 copies still are unaccounted for.

In 1914, Judge Leon Montes, a specialist of Haitian stamps, walked into a post office in Port-au-Prince, Haiti, to purchase stamps from the newly overprinted series. He bought a strip of 10, unaware that these stamps would become Haiti's greatest rarities.

On February 7, 1914, General Oreste Zamor overthrew the administration of President Michel Oreste and was elected president of Haiti the following day. To honor its new president, Haiti overprinted stamps with the inscription, "GL.O.Z. 7 Fev. 1914."

These were the overprinted stamps that Judge Montes intended to buy at the Port-au-Prince post office. Thousands of these overprinted stamps were issued. They are common today.

But the strip of 10 50-centime stamps that Judge Montes purchased bore an additional overprint, "Poste Paye." The postal clerk tore the strip from the bottom of a pane of 50. When the judge examined the stamps that evening, he noticed the additional handstamp. He realized that these stamps differed from the normal commemorative overprints. When he returned to the post office the next day to buy the remainder of the pane, he found that it was no longer available. The postal clerk speculated that it had been sold to another stamp collector, a Mr. Baptiste, then consul of the United States in Haiti. This turned out not to be true.

In the 1974 *Congress Book*, published by the American Philatelic Congress, F. Burton Sellers said it was likely the remaining 40 stamps were returned to the National Bank for storage. According to Sellers, Everett A. Colson, a noted collector of Haitian stamps in the early years of this century, was sent to Haiti in 1919 by the United States Government as a financial adviser. Using his position, Colson contacted the director of the National Bank and obtained a copy of the inventory for September 1914 of stamp stocks in the National Bank. The inventory indicated that the bank held 40 copies of the 50c "GL.O.Z." stamps with the two overprints.

Colson later reported to another collector, Dr. Clarence W. Hennan, that he actually saw the 40 stamps in the bank safe in 1919.

To understand the scarcity of these stamps, it is necessary to know the background of the basic stamp. Haiti issued the basic 50c stamp in 1904 as part of a six-value set depicting President Pedro Nord-Alexis. The stamp is listed in the Scott catalog as number 101. This set was issued concurrently with another set celebrating the centenary of Haiti's independence.

Sellers said it is generally accepted that both issues were paid for by a wealthy Haitian, M. Borno, in exchange for which he received a quantity of the stamps. When Borno began using the stamps on his correspondence and selling them to dealers and collectors, the Haitian postal authorities tried to put a stop to it.

The authorities overprinted the government stocks with the inscription "Poste Paye 1804-1904." The only stamps from these sets that were valid for postage were those bearing this overprint. Two types of overprint exist: one large, the other small.

The overprint transformed the 50c Nord-Alexis stamp into Scott 107. Only the small overprint was used for this value.

Haiti overprinted the remainders of the Nord-Alexis series (Scott 96-101) with the "GL.O.Z." overprint in 1914, producing Scott 170-75. Included in these stocks was at least one pane of the 50c with

61

the "Poste Paye" overprint. Two types of the "GL.O.Z." overprint also exist. Type I is distinguished by a short foot of the "L" of "GL." Also the "1" in "1914" has the period directly above it. Type II is characterized by a long foot of the "L." The "1" of "1914" is to the right of the period above.

When the stamps were overprinted, they should have been returned to the National Bank for audit and storage. Records show, however, that several thousand of all values were sold directly to the post office without being returned to the National Bank for audit. Apparently, the pane of 50c stamps with the two overprints was among those sold directly to the post office. The remainder of the pane probably was returned to the National Bank after Montes purchased his 10 copies.

In the 1974 *Congress Book*, Sellers recorded the provenance for seven of the 10 copies. Three of the seven were genuinely used. One is on piece and is canceled February 27, 1914, in Port-au-Prince. A second used copy was removed from this piece. The third used copy was canceled the same day in Port-au-Prince. The three probably were used on covers created by Judge Montes. He frequently mailed covers bearing new issues to himself or his wife.

In the 1974 *Congress Book*, Sellers requested information on the eighth, ninth and tenth copies of the rarity. No information was forthcoming until 1976 when Sellers picked up a copy of the May 4-6 Harmer, Rooke auction catalog. The auction featured the Edmond Mangones collection of Haiti. The front cover of the catalog pictured the copy of the stamp referred to by Sellers as number 9 (after Judge Montes' original ascription). Although referred to as number 9, the stamp actually is the eighth to be located.

Two copies remain a mystery. Sellers said the copy labeled number 8 originally was given to Louis Soray of Haiti. Soray said many years ago that he mislaid the stamp.

The copy labeled number 10 originally was given by Judge Montes to a Mr. Monnereau. Following Monnereau's death, it was sold to a Mr. Buteau of Port-au-Prince. Buteau later sold it to Edmond Mangones, who also owned copy number 9. Mangones sold copy number 10 to Carlo Jaeger, who later sold it to a publishing house in Port-au-Prince. Its current whereabouts are unknown.

The Scott catalog lists this Haitian rarity at $3,000 mint or used. The relatively low price can be attributed in part to the unpopularity of Haiti as a collecting country.

Collectors should be aware that counterfeits exist. The infamous Raoul de Thuin created fakes of this issue. However, as Sellers explained, de Thuin's cliche of the "GL.O.Z." overprint was of type I, which does not exist on the rarity. He also used the large-letters type of "Poste Paye" overprint. Only the small-letters type appears on the genuine stamp. Other crudely produced fakes exist. Collectors should have these stamps expertized.

Up In Smoke

VALUE: $9,350
This 1893 6¢ green stamp of Hawaii received a black overprint instead of the red overprint as intended.

The San Francisco earthquake of 1906 claimed as its victims several rare stamps. **Philatelic Gems 2** told the story of the Japanese 1874 20-sen syllabic character 1 stamp that was destroyed, along with other rarities that were in the Henry J. Crocker collection, when the earthquake devastated San Francisco. The earthquake also forced stamp dealer J.H. Makins out of business when it destroyed his stock, including copies of two Hawaiian rarities.

In 1893, a revolution led by nine Americans, two Britons and two Germans deposed Hawaii's Queen Liliuokalani. A provisional government was set up. In 1894, the government proclaimed Hawaii a republic headed by Sanford B. Dole.

The provisional government overprinted Hawaii's stamps and postal stationery with the inscription "Provisional/GOVT/1893" in three lines. The Hawaiian Gazette Company applied the overprint in red or black ink, depending on the color of the basic stamp. Light-colored stamps were overprinted in black; dark-colored stamps in red. About 3.5 million overprinted stamps were created.

Two major errors exist among these provisionals. One sheet of 50 6¢ green Kamehameha V stamps were overprinted in black, instead of the intended red. Similarly, one sheet of the 10¢ red-brown David Kalakaua received a red overprint, instead of black.

In 1901, stamp dealer J.H. Makins traveled to Hawaii to buy stamps. A stamp collector gave Makins a tip: Messrs. Thrum & Company, a stationery company in Honolulu, owned most of the 10¢ red-brown with the erroneous red overprint. Makins said the stationery company had purchased the stamps from a small post office outside Honolulu. Thrum & Company, not being in the stamp

VALUE: $5,060

This 10¢ stamp received a red overprint instead of the intended black.

business, had no idea of the true value of these stamps. Makins bought 35 copies of the error.

Another tip led Makins to Joseph M. Oat, the postmaster general of Hawaii. Oat had 36 copies of the 6¢ green with the black overprint error. Makins purchased all of these.

However, these stamps were not the bargain that the 10¢ errors had been. Oats was well-aware that the stamps were errors and were valuable. Makins said he invested "some considerable quantity of cash" in the stamps. He said that Oat gave him an affidavit stating that the 6¢ with the black overprint was a genuine error and had been regularly issued to the post office at Honolulu. He claimed it was this affidavit that later convinced Scott Publishing Company to list the overprint errors in its catalog.

He then learned that L.T. Kenake, an employee of the Honolulu Post Office, had 10 copies of the 6¢ error. Makins also purchased these. In a very short period of time, Makins had cornered the market on the overprint errors. He began selling copies.

In 1906, however, his luck ran out. Makins' business, Makins & Company, was located in San Francisco. In April of that year, an earthquake shook San Francisco, and the fire that followed devastated the city. This catastrophe claimed 452 lives and caused more than $300 million damage. Among its casualties were several rare stamps owned by collectors and dealers living in San Francisco.

Makins' office was located on the second floor of a building whose basement was occupied by a wholesale liquor distributor. Makins estimated that eight copies of the 10¢ error and 10 copies of the 6¢ were locked in a safe, along with the rest of his stock, on the second floor. During the earthquake, the floors collapsed, and the safe fell into the basement, buried by the bricks and rubble. The whiskeys and wines exploded, creating a monstrous fire. The safe — red hot from the fire — could not be touched for weeks.

Makins finally secured a permit to uncover the safe. When he opened its door, the contents burst into flames. His stock — including the Hawaiian rarities — was destroyed.

Makins told his story in *Weekly Philatelic Gossip* in 1936. He was no longer a stamp dealer. He had been put out of business by the earthquake and fire.

The Scott catalog lists the 6¢ overprint error at $16,500 mint. The 10¢ error catalogs at $16,500 mint and $17,500 used.

At its February 1-3, 1984, auction, Richard A. Wolffers Inc. sold an example of the 10¢ overprint error for $8,800. Daniel F. Kelleher Inc. sold one copy of each error at its September 30-October 1, 1986, auction. The 6¢ realized $7,975; the 10¢ $11,000. At Christie's October 30, 1986, a copy of the 6¢ sold for $9,350; a 10¢ brought $5,060. Prices include a 10-percent buyer's premium.

66

INDIA

Two-Sided Stamp

VALUE: $3,960

This used India ½-anna stamp of 1854 is printed on both sides. The impression on the reverse side of the stamp is shown at right.

One of the most interesting stamps of India is the 1854 ½-anna blue. Three dies can be distinguished, and retouches and varieties abound. But the most interesting variety is also one of India's great rarities. A copy of the stamp exists printed on both sides.

Captain H.L. Thuillier printed the first general issues of India. Captain Thuillier was deputy surveyor-general in charge of the Lithographic Department of the Survey Office in Calcutta, India. He took his new assignment seriously and began experimenting in the printing of these stamps. He tried several inks and colors. Captain Thuillier produced a ½-anna red stamp, but this was never issued.

An Indian artist, Numerodeen, prepared the copper plate from which transfers were taken and lithographic stones were produced. Captain Thuillier then printed the ½-anna stamp in blue.

The stones deteriorated from prolonged printing. Three dies were used for this stamp. Jal Cooper discusses the distinguishing characteristics of these dies in his book *Stamps of India*.

Stamp collectors had studied the varieties of this ½-anna stamp for several years. But in 1931 a new discovery was made. A collector found a copy of the stamp printed on both sides. This stamp is used. The impression on the reverse is light but distinguishable. It shows about half the stamp design, including a portion of the corner ornament and the frame of an adjoining stamp at right.

H.R. Harmer Company sold this rarity for the first time in its January 11, 1932, sale. It realized £26. Harmers again offered the stamp in its October 12, 1954, sale where it sold for £230.

The stamp came up for sale when Harmers of London offered it in its May 10, 1988, auction. It realized $3,960, including the 10-percent buyer's premium. The Scott catalog lists the stamp as number 2b and prices it at $7,500.

Cooper said the impression on the reverse may be due to the sheet being carelessly rested on the stone.

More Than Cheese

VALUE: $49,500
One of only seven recorded tete-beche pairs of Parma's 1852 15-centesimo stamp franks this 1853 entire to Marc Antonio Serra in Genoa.

Parma is better known for its sharp-flavored cheese than for its stamps. This Italian state, however, does boast one extremely scarce error — the 1852 15-centesimo tete-beche pair.

In 1840, when the world's first adhesive postage stamp was issued by Great Britain, Italy was divided into several political spheres known as the Italian states. These included the Kingdom of Sardinia, which ruled the island of Sardinia and northwestern Italy; the Kingdom of Lombardy-Venetia, which was ruled by Austria in the north; the Papal States, which controlled the central portion of the peninsula; and the Kingdom of the Two Sicilies in the south. Other states included the Grand Duchy of Tuscany in west-central Italy and the northern duchies of Parma and Modena.

At the time of the release of the Penny Black, the Italian states followed various political allegiances. For example, Sardinia had close ties with France. On the other hand, Parma, along with Lombardy-Venetia, Modena and Tuscany, associated closely with Austria. These political associations were reflected in the stamp issues of the Italian states.

When the Austro-Italian Postal League was formed in 1851, Lombardy-Venetia, Modena, Tuscany and Parma joined. One of the requirements of membership was that each state use stamps to designate prepayment of postage.

The duchy of Parma introduced its first postage stamps in 1852. The set consists of 5c, 10c, 15c, 25c and 40c denominations, each featuring a crown and fleur-de-lis design. Donnino Bentelli engraved this issue. Stefano Rossi-Ubaldi typographed the stamps at his printing house in Parma.

During the printing of the 15c, the cliche in the ninth position in the sheet of 80 was inserted upside down. This created tete-beche pairs. In a tete-beche pair, one stamp is upside down, or inverted, in relation to the other.

The error was quickly corrected. Only seven tete-beche pairs have been recorded. They seldom come up for sale.

In 1986, however, a spectacular item was offered in the November 20-21 auction conducted by Phillips in England. This item was an entire letter from Parma to Genoa bearing the 15c tete-beche pair used in 1853. The entire is accompanied by an Enzo Diena certificate stating: "The copy with sheet margin is the inverted one, no. (9) of the lower-left pane of the setting."

This rarity realized £33,000 (about $49,500), including a 10-percent buyer's premium. The Scott catalog lists the 15c tete-beche pairs at $60,000.

ITALY

An Overlooked Error

VALUE: $32,800

One of the two known copies of Italy's 1865 20-centesimo-on-15c stamp with the surcharge inverted.

The search for rarities is an ongoing process for stamp collectors. This was shown most recently with the Candleholder invert of the United States. Collectors all over the world are searching for the remaining inverts — or another pane.

An Italian invert led to a similar search in the past. A rate hike led to the creation of what was to become one of the scarcest stamps of the Republic of Italy. Only two examples have been recorded, but at least 100 were produced. Where are the remaining 98?

In 1864, Italy increased its postal rates. A new 20-centesimo value was needed to cover this rate. Costantino Perazzi, an official of Italy's Ministry of Finance, sent a telegram to the printer, Thomas De La Rue, asking that the production of all other Italian stamps be halted. De La Rue was to devote all its efforts to printing the new 20c stamps. Perazzi reconsidered and decided instead to surcharge existing stocks of the then current 15c King Victor Emmanuel II stamp with the new 20c value.

The 20c-on-15c dull blue stamps were released in 1865. The

71

brown surcharge consists of an oval with "20 C," which appears at the bottom of the stamp, and "C 20," which appears in the upper corners of the stamp.

Three types of stamps were surcharged. Type I features white dots flanking the stars in the oval, and a dot in the eight checkmark ornaments in the corners. Type II consists of dots in the oval, but none in the corners. Type III shows no dots at all.

Most catalogs credit De La Rue with the printing of these surcharges. However, in his handbook, *Italian Stamps*, Roy A. Dehn disagreed. He said that since the surcharged provisional was not replaced by a regular 20c stamp for more than two years, the 10 million or so stamps printed by De La Rue would not have lasted. Dehn said, "I calculate that the annual consumption of this important value must have exceeded 40 million. Unless earlier deliveries were shipped back to England for overprinting, of which there seems to be no evidence, the majority of the provisionals must have been overprinted in Turin."

At least one pane of 100 stamps received the surcharge upside down. Only two examples of this inverted surcharge have been discovered. These are among the scarcest and most valuable stamps of the Republic of Italy.

At its November 18-20, 1986, auction, Harmers of London sold one of the two stamps with the inverted surcharge for £23,100 (about $32,800). In an unprecedented attempt to locate additional copies of the error, Bernard Harmer, chairman of Harmers, offered to donate £2,500 to the favorite charity of anyone discovering another copy of the 1865 20c-on-15c with the surcharge inverted. The only stipulation was that the newly discovered copy would have to be sold through either the London or New York Harmer galleries.

Harmer expressed surprise that none of the remaining 98 examples had been discovered. "It is not a very obvious error, as the dull blue color of the stamp itself might result in the error being overlooked," he said. Yet, almost a year after Harmer's offer, no additional copies have been reported.

The Scott catalog lists the error at $30,000.

ITALY (Ottoman Empire)

Italians In Turkey

VALUE: $32,000

Only eight copies have been recorded of this unissued 1922 15-piaster-on-25-centesimo stamp of the Italian Offices in the Ottoman Empire.

An unissued stamp from the Italian Offices in the Ottoman Empire ranks as one of the great airmail rarities of the world.

Various powers maintained post offices in the Ottoman Empire prior to World War I. These post offices were authorized by treaties and continued in operation throughout the war. The Ottoman Empire consisted of countries bordering on the eastern Mediterranean. Italy began issuing stamps for its offices in the empire in 1908, surcharging its own contemporary issues for use in the area. Specific issues for use in specific areas of the empire appeared as early as 1901.

In 1922, a time when aviation was coming into its own, a flight was planned from Bucharest to Paris. The Italian Post Office in the Ottoman Empire arranged to have mail carried by train from Constantinople to Bucharest and then by plane to Paris.

The post office ordered the surcharging of Italy's 25-centesimo special delivery stamp of the 1903-26 series. The stamp portrays Victor Emmanuel III at the left with "ESPRESSO" in large letters to the right. This stamp was surcharged with a 15-piaster value and overprinted with a large airplane. The inscription "SERVIZIO POSTAL AEREO" appears above the plane.

At the same time the stamps were coming off the presses, world

73

leaders were meeting in Lausanne, Switzerland, to decide the fate of the Ottoman Empire. Little did these leaders realize, or perhaps even care, that their decisions would affect a stamp issue and create a rarity.

In relinquishing their rights to the empire, the allied powers agreed to close all foreign post offices in the area. The Italian Post Office ordered its offices closed and withdrew the airmail issue for the Bucharest-Paris flight prior to the stamp's release. The post office further ordered the printing destroyed, except for three copies that were to be preserved for the post office archives.

Apparently, more than three copies were saved from destruction. Today, eight exist. Six of these contain the overprint inscription with the spelling "POSTALE." Two are known with the spelling "POSTAL." Harmers of London sold a copy with the "POSTALE" spelling in 1986 by tender. Collector Giangiacomo Orlandini of Switzerland paid £21,202 (about $32,000) for the stamp.

In 1920, the Treaty of Sevres granted independence to parts of the Ottoman Empire and gave other parts to various Allied powers. Turkey was formally proclaimed a republic on October 29, 1923.

LAGOS

An Unintentional Surcharge

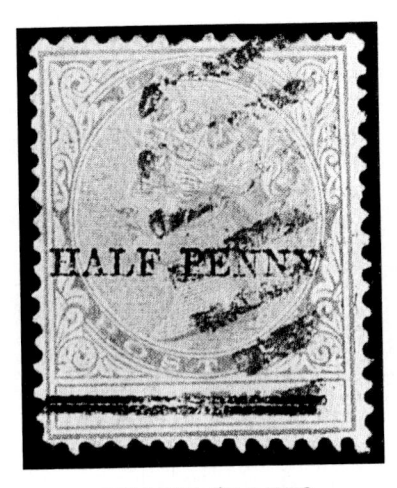

VALUE: $11,550
The discovery copy of the ½-penny-on-2d surcharge error from Lagos.

Little is known of a philatelic gem from Lagos, a former British crown colony in West Africa.

The British became involved in the affairs of Lagos in the 1850s when they captured the territory in an attempt to halt slave trade. The British navy restored a deposed monarch to the throne in 1851 and established a consulate in Lagos in 1853. The territory was annexed by Great Britain in 1861 and placed under the control of the governor of Sierra Leone. Lagos remained part of Great Britain's West African settlements from 1866 to 1874, when it became part of the Gold Coast Colony.

In 1874, Lagos issued its first stamps. This set featured the portrait of Queen Victoria and is regarded as the forerunner of the colonial keyplates, since the same design also was used for the stamps of St. Christopher and Tobago.

Lagos continued to use this design throughout its stamp-issuing history. Values were added to the series and the color of the

75

stamps were changed, but the design remained the same.

In 1893, however, the territory experienced a shortage of ½-penny stamps. Little is known of what led up to this shortage. What is known is that a great rarity was one of the results.

The postal officials in Lagos authorized the surcharging of the 4d lilac-and-black stamp with the inscription "HALF PENNY." While the 4d stamps were being surcharged, the printer mistakenly picked up a sheet of the 2d stamps and put it through the press, leading to the creation of the ½d-on-2d surcharge error. There was never any intention to surcharge the 2d stamps.

Nevile Lacy Stocken, author of *Stamps of Great Price*, discovered the first copy of this Lagos surcharge error in 1936. This is the only known used copy. Stocken's discovery was the only recorded example of this error until 1952 when a dealer discovered an unused example in a stamp collection. No other copies of this error have been recorded.

Colonel J.R. Danson bought the used copy discovered by Stocken. It changed hands again when Christie's sold the stamp for $11,550, including a 10-percent buyer's premium, at its March 11, 1987, Isleham sale. The Scott catalog lists this rarity unpriced.

Lagos issued its last stamps in 1902. In 1906, Lagos and Southern Nigeria were united into the Protectorate of Southern Nigeria. When Northern and Southern Nigeria were united as the Protectorate of Nigeria in 1914, Lagos was made its capital. Today, Lagos is a state of Nigeria. The city of Lagos is Nigeria's capital.

MALTA

Jumped the Gun

VALUE: $3,190

Only 1,530 copies of this 10/- of 1919 were produced. All sold out quickly.

The rarest of Malta's stamps is the 10/- black of 1919. This stamp is part of a pictorial series first issued in 1899.

The 10/- design, showing St. Paul after the shipwreck, was first used in 1899. The stamp was engraved by Thomas De La Rue of England and printed on Crown and CC watermarked paper.

In 1919, the design was altered slightly to include the inscriptions "Postage" and "Revenue." The new 10/- was printed on Multiple Crown CA watermarked paper. But this new stamp was not intended for release until the supplies of the earlier 10/- stamps had been exhausted. However, the post office jumped the gun and issued the new 10/- early. Only 51 sheets of 30 of this stamp (1,530 total) were printed. All were sold out in a few days, which accounts for the stamp's scarcity.

Why such a small printing? The book, *Malta: The Postal History & Postage Stamps 1576-1960*, published by the Malta Study Circle, states that this may have been a token printing. The postmaster of

Valetta at the time the stamp was issued has been quoted as saying the stamp was issued prematurely.

The Malta book refers to an article in the December 15, 1921, *Philatelic Magazine*, which states: "The issue in 1919 of the new 10/- stamp inscribed 'POSTAGE' and 'REVENUE' and watermark Multiple Crown CA and the reissue of the old design on CC paper has given rise to some misconceptions. "It has been freely stated that the Multiple Crown CA stamps were issued in error, and withdrawn from sale until the CC stamps were exhausted, when they would again be placed on sale; but as a new supply on CA paper had been ordered, we wrote to the Post Master of Malta to clear up the point. In reply he informs us that a small stock of 10/- stamps on CA paper was issued by mistake and were completely sold out. Since then only the CC stamps have been available and the stock of these is expected to last until September 1922 when the new CS stamps which have arrived will be issued."

Apparently, a surplus of the 10/- on Crown and CC watermarked paper did exist. The 10/- on Multiple CA paper was not to be released until the former stock had been exhausted. The stamps on Multiple CA paper were sold out within a few days, and the stamps on the Crown CC watermarked paper were once again placed on sale.

The value of the 10/- on Multiple CA paper has rapidly increased over the years. In 1920-21, it was selling for about $15. Today, Scott catalog prices it at $6,000 mint and $8,000 used. Prices realized during the past few years have ranged from $1,200 for an imperfect copy to $3,300. Harmers of New York sold a copy of this rarity for $3,190, including a 10-percent buyer's premium, at its October 28-29, 1986, auction.

A Colonial Surcharge

VALUE: $4,125
Only 25 copies were produced of this 1886-91 5-centime-on-20c stamp overprinted "MARTINIQUE."

VALUE: $3,850
Just 50 15c-on-4c surcharged stamps of 1886-91 were printed for the French colony of Martinique.

Two outstanding rarities come from the former French colony of Martinique. This island in the West Indies began issuing its own stamps in 1886. The first series of Martinique stamps consisted of the French Colonies stamps overprinted "MARTINIQUE" and surcharged with a new value: 1 centime, 5c or 15c. These denominations covered the basic postal rates used by the island.

The stamps were crudely surcharged on the island by the Government Printer of Fort-de-France. Several types of surcharges were used. These are illustrated in the Scott catalog.

Many varieties resulted from the crude printings, including inverted surcharges, double surcharges, and slanting numerals. While some of these are scarce, the true gems of Martinique owe their scarcity to low printing totals rather than errors.

Only 25 copies of the 5c-on-20c stamp with type B surcharge were produced. The Scott catalog lists both mint and used copies at $13,000. John W. Kaufmann Inc. auctioned a used copy at its May 14, 1986, sale. The stamp realized $4,125, including the 10-percent buyer's premium.

Only 50 copies of the 15c-on-4c stamp were produced. Scott lists this rarity at $11,000 mint, $10,000 used. The May 14, 1986, Kaufmann auction also featured an example of this stamp. It realized $3,850, including the 10-percent buyer's premium.

The low prices can be attributed in part to the lack of interest in the stamps of Martinique. But no one can deny the scarcity of these two issues. Few survive today.

Foot To Foot

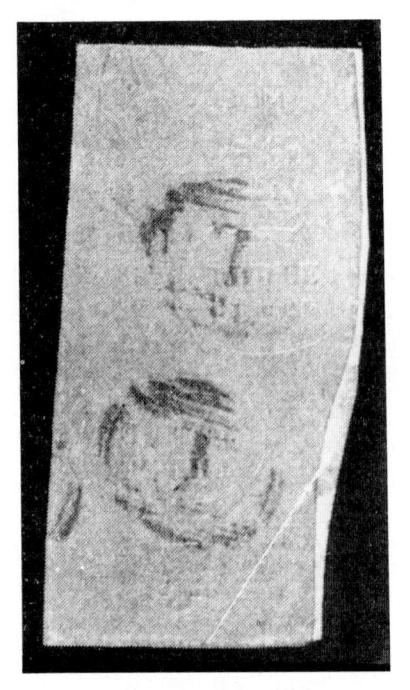

VALUE: $17,500
The tete-beche pairs are the scarcest varieties of Natal's first issue.

Natal's first stamps are among the scarcest in the world, but one variety stands out among the others. Only seven examples exist of the 3-penny tete-beche variety of 1857.

The government of Natal decided to issue adhesive stamps in 1857. While the government awaited the arrival of the regular stamps from England, it issued a set of provisionals. These provisionals are most unusual. F. Davis and Sons, a local printer in Pietermaritzburg, produced the stamps on paper that resembled blotting paper. The result is that the stamps are crudely embossed. The design, which consists of a crown, the initials "VR"

(Victoria Regina) and the value, is barely visible on most of these stamps. The printer had access to several colors of this blotting paper; the stamps were printed in rose, green, blue and buff.

The towns of Durban and Pietermaritzburg were sparsely populated. Few people wrote letters, so the need for stamps was limited. Since there was little demand, the printer produced limited quantities of these provisionals, contributing to their scarcity. The stamps were imperforate, making it necessary for users to cut them apart. Many of the stamps were destroyed when they were cut apart, again contributing to their scarcity.

Despite the obvious limitations, the printer produced surprisingly few varieties. The 3d tete-beche variety is perhaps the best known.

H.R. Holmes traced the whereabouts of the seven tete-beche pairs in the *London Philatelist*, the journal of the Royal Philatelic Society of London. The Royal Collection at Buckingham Palace has a pair with the embossed impressions foot to foot. The stamps are canceled with a circular datestamp "22 AP/NATAL" in blue. Count Ferrari once owned this pair.

Holmes noted that the Thomas K. Tapling collection in the British Library contains a pair canceled with the circular datestamp "1 DE/NATAL." The two impressions are foot to foot.

Another pair with the impressions embossed foot to foot is in the H.H. Hurst collection at the Durban Museum in South Africa. This is canceled "1" in block. This pair was owned by Norman Welsford.

The Royal Philatelic Society of London owns a pair also canceled "1" in black. This pair was in the Henry J. Duveen, Arthur Hind, Carlton Jones and E.W. Mann collections. The Mann collection is now the property of the RPSL.

The only copy on cover was sold by David Feldman SA during its November 19-23, 1985, auction in New York City. The cover is addressed to "The Very Reverend the Dean of Pietermaritzburg." The pair is pen canceled with an "X." The cover realized $13,800, including a 15-percent buyer's premium, at the Feldman auction.

William H. Crocker owned a pair that was sold by Harmer, Rooke in London in 1938. It is canceled with a "1" in black. Colonel E.H.R. Green also owned an example that was sold by H.C. Barr in New York in 1945. Holmes said this pair is cut to an oval shape and is canceled in black "POST OFFICE-P. M. BURG." The whereabouts of the Crocker and Green copies are unknown at this time.

The Scott catalog lists the variety as 1a and prices it at $17,500.

Indigo-Blue Rarity

VALUE: $2,200
A copy of Nauru's overprinted issue, the 10/- indigo blue of 1916-23.

A great rarity comes from the world's smallest nation, Nauru. This eight-square-mile island is located in the central Pacific Ocean between the Marshall and Solomon islands. Nauru was a German possession from 1888 to 1914 and was occupied by Australian forces during World War I. The island was mandated to the British Empire following World War I and was administered jointly by Great Britain, New Zealand and Australia.

From 1916 to 1923, Nauru used British stamps overprinted with the island's name. Few people resided on the island, and there was little demand for stamps.

Small quantities of Great Britain's 1912-13 King George V definitives were overprinted "NAURU" by the Stamp Department of the Board of Inland Revenue in London. The lower values — ½ penny through 1/- — were overprinted in block capitals. The 2/6d, 6/- and 10/- high values were overprinted in Roman capitals. The high values feature the famous "Britannia Rules the Waves" scene with the portrait of George V to the left.

Four different printers produced Britain's George V high values — Waterlow Brothers and Layton, De La Rue and Company, Bradbury, Wilkinson and Company, and Waterlow and Sons.

Nauru's 10/- rarity results from these different printings. Stamps from two of these printers — De La Rue, and Waterlow Brothers and Layton — were overprinted for use on Nauru. The De La Rue printings were by far the most commonly used for the Nauru overprints. Although the Waterlow printings of the 2/6d and 6/- bring substantially higher prices than the De La Rue printings of those values, the gem of Nauru is the 10/- Waterlow printing.

The most noticeable characteristics of these printings are the colors. The De La Rue 10/- is printed in light blue; the Waterlow printing is in indigo blue. It is this indigo-blue stamp that is extremely rare. The Scott catalog prices this rarity at $10,000.

Harmers of New York sold a used copy of this stamp at its September 16-17, 1986, auction. It realized $2,200, including the 10-percent buyer's premium. At its 1987 Rarities of the World sale, Robert A. Siegel Auction Galleries sold a used copy for $1,925, including the 10-percent buyer's premium.

Unauthorized Bisects

VALUE: $20,000

A bisect of the New Brunswick 1/- dull violet franks this cover addressed to Boston. The stamp pays the 6-penny rate to the United States.

    Among the great rarities of British North America is New Brunswick's 1/- stamp of 1851 and the bisects of this issue.
    New Brunswick achieved postal independence in 1851 and wasted no time in issuing stamps. Its first issue, known as the Pence issue, went on sale at post offices on September 6 of that year. The set consisted of 3-penny, 6d and 1/- denominations.
    Each of the diamond-shaped stamps featured a design common to the set, showing the crown of Great Britain in the center surrounded by roses at the top and bottom, a shamrock to the left and thistle to the right. These heraldic flowers symbolized England, Ireland and Scotland.
    The most valuable of these stamps is the 1/-. Two printings exist — one in bright red-violet; the other in dull violet. Mint copies of this value are extremely rare. The Scott catalog lists the 1/- bright red-violet at $12,500 mint, $3,250 used, and the dull-violet shade at

85

$11,500 mint and $3,750 used. A mint example of the 1/- dull violet is in the Royal Collection in Buckingham Palace.

Exceedingly rare are the bisects of New Brunswick's first issue.

On August 1, 1854, the New Brunswick Post Office reduced the postal rate to England from 1/3d to 7½d. The three existing stamps — 3d, 6d and 1/- — could not be used to make up this rate.

In *The Postage Stamps of New Brunswick and Nova Scotia*, author Nicholas Argenti explains that Nova Scotia was experiencing a similar problem at this time, and the postmaster general of that

VALUE: Indeterminable

This copy of the New Brunswick 1/- dull violet is in the Royal Collection.

province authorized the bisecting of the 3d stamp to be used as a 1½d stamp. The 3d was to be cut in half diagonally. Only the 3d was to be used for this purpose.

The New Brunswick postmaster general, however, gave no such authorization. Nonetheless, the residents of New Brunswick, taking their cue from Nova Scotia, began bisecting their three stamps — not only diagonally, but also horizontally and vertically. They also cut the 1/- in quarters for the 3d rate and similarly cut the 6d for a 1½d and 3d for a ½d.

These cutup copies of New Brunswick's first issue rank among the true gems of British North America.

The bisect of the 3d on cover is listed in the Scott catalog at $3,500. The bisect of the 6d catalogs at $3,750. A quarter of this stamp, however, is listed at $17,500.

Scott lists the bisect and quarter of the 1/- bright red-violet on cover, but gives no prices. The bisect and quarter of the 1/- dull violet used on cover catalog at $20,000 each.

At its September 24-28, 1979, auction in Zurich, David Feldman SA sold a superb cover bearing the 1/- dull violet bisect paying the 6d rate to the United States. It realized 48,000 Swiss francs.

Feldman sold a folded cover from Chatham to Moncton bearing the 1851 6d and 1/- bright red-violet at its November 19-23, 1985, auction in New York City. The cover realized $17,250, including a 15-percent buyer's premium.

When Harmers of New York sold the specialized New Brunswick collection on October 29, 1986, several covers bearing the 1/- were auctioned. Another cover with a bisect of the 1/- dull violet realized $18,700, including a 10-percent buyer's premium, at this sale. This cover was formerly in the Ferrari and Dale-Lichtenstein collections.

A cover bearing a quarter of the 1/- dull mauve used as a 3d sold for $13,200, including a 10-percent buyer's premium.

A Show Rarity

VALUE: $10,000
A spectacular block of four of the New Zealand 1-penny claret of 1906.

Stamp collectors who attended an industrial exhibition in New Zealand in 1906 were unaware that a rarity was within their reach. One sheet of the scarce 1-penny claret from the Christchurch Exhibition issue was on sale at the show, but few collectors realized it.

While the citizens of Christchurch prepared for New Zealand's first international trade exhibition, the New Zealand Post Office prepared its first set of commemoratives to promote the show.

The Post Office selected designs by Auckland artist L.J. Steel. The designs had been submitted for a previous issue but had not been used. They show the arrival of the Maoris (½d), Maori art (1d), landing of Captain Cook (3d) and annexation of New Zealand (6d).

Several problems occurred during the production of these four stamps. While it was originally proposed that all four stamps be printed in single colors, the designs for the 3d and 6d required two colors. The New Zealand Government Printing Office experimented by preparing essays using photolithography, but these proved to be unsuitable. Trial printings also were taken from zinc and copper plates, but these also were rejected. The printer finally used dies engraved by W.R. Bock to create electrotype plates. The stamps were typographed in sheets consisting of two panes of 30.

In selecting the colors, the Post Office chose claret for the 1d. Four thousand sheets were printed in the claret shade before the Post Office realized that the color was too dark to do justice to the design. The Post Office stopped the printing of the sheets of the claret stamps and ordered the stamps reprinted in vermilion.

One sheet of the claret stamps was sent to the postmaster general. The Post Office retained 14 sheets for its archives. A few of the stamps were given to dignitaries.

But unknown to stamp collectors, one sheet was given to the exhibition to be placed on sale at the show.

In their book, *The Postage Stamps of New Zealand*, R.J.G. Collins and H.T.M. Fathers said that one visitor to the show bought six copies of the 1d claret and used them daily on letters to his wife in Wellington. When he purchased a copy of the 1d vermilion, he realized that he may have a rarity. He returned to the post office substation but found that only the vermilion shade was available.

Collins and Fathers said that the clerk at the substation recalled that the sheet of claret stamps was on top of the bundle she received for sale on the first day. She said, however, that sales of the Christchurch Exhibition stamps were limited to six per person at the show. Therefore, no person at the show could have received more than six of the 1d claret at one time.

Today, the claret stamp is one of New Zealand's great rarities. The Scott catalog lists it at $10,000 mint and $12,500 used.

In 1986, the New Zealand Post Office consigned a gutter block of four of this rare stamp to New Zealand auctioneer Len Jury. Proceeds from the sale of the block were to aid another exhibition — this time an international stamp show scheduled for 1990 in New Zealand. The block, however, was withdrawn at the auction when the highest bid was less than half the hoped for NZ$100,000.

NEW ZEALAND

Train With No Value

VALUE: $750

The 1963 New Zealand 1/9d value with the red color omitted, affecting the value and train, is shown at left. The normal stamp appears at right.

A theft has added to the intrigue surrounding a New Zealand error. In 1963, New Zealand issued 3-penny and 1-shilling 9-penny stamps marking the centenary of the country's railways.

A collector purchased a sheet of 120 of the 1/9d stamp at a small New Zealand post office. When he returned home, he immediately noticed that the red color was missing. The stamp had no value marking, and the red color of the train was omitted.

The collector contacted Bridger & Kay Ltd., stamp dealers in London. Recognizing the popularity of such errors at that time, Bridger & Kay purchased the sheet. They removed the top right-hand block of four, which has since been broken up, and 12 singles from the sheet.

A short time later, thieves broke into the dealers' premises and stole the remainder of the sheet. Only the 16 copies removed from the sheet have appeared on the market in recent years.

Allan Leverton, director of Bridger & Kay, says other stamps from the sheet could be identified from a photograph of the sheet, which he possesses. He says any copies with left-hand or lower margins or imprints were stolen.

Although only 16 copies have appeared on the market, the catalog value is not as high as might be expected. Scott catalog lists it at $750. The 3d of this set also has been discovered with blue omitted, affecting the sky. Scott lists this error at $300.

Printed On Notepaper

VALUE: $13,750
This copy of the Newfoundland 1860 1/- orange stamp on vertically laid paper was in the Count Ferrari and Dale-Lichtenstein collections.

With all the precautions taken in printing stamps, imagine a stamp printed on ordinary notepaper. One of the great rarities of Newfoundland is believed to have been printed on just that — common notepaper. Newfoundland's 1860 1-shilling orange on laid paper intrigues collectors. Fewer than 10 copies exist. While many speculate about the origins of this stamp, no one is quite sure how it came into being.

What collectors do know is that only three have been recorded on vertically laid paper and one on horizontally laid paper. These copies have resided in some of the greatest collections of all times, including the collections of Count Ferrari, Alfred Lichtenstein, and King Carol of Romania.

Robert H. Pratt spent many years studying the pence issues of Newfoundland, which included the 1/- orange. Following much research into the origins of the 1/- orange on laid paper, Pratt concluded that the stamps are proofs. Even so, he admitted that the printing of stamps or proofs on laid paper is unusual.

In his book, *The Pence Issues of Newfoundland 1857-1866*, he said that only one other Newfoundland stamp is known on laid paper of the same type. That is a 2-penny black, which evidently was cut from some advertising piece.

Although it is unusual for stamps to be printed on laid paper, which is now commonly used as notepaper, it is not difficult to imagine finding large quantities of this type of paper in any press room. Pratt theorized that the printer ran off proofs to test the color or plate of the 1/- orange stamp.

Another mystery unfolds involving these laid-paper stamps. Of the laid-paper examples known, only one is on horizontally laid paper. When two vertically laid examples were compared at the ANPHILEX international stamp show in New York in 1971, it was found that they were a matched pair that at one time had been joined together. A single copy, which was sold in 1969 when H.R. Harmer auctioned the Dale-Lichtenstein collection, seems to have been joined to this pair, according to Pratt.

What then is the origin of the unique copy on horizontally laid paper? Pratt believes it to be a die proof.

In his book, he explained, "Orientation of a piece of notepaper beneath a die or plate could be random, but would logically be parallel or at right angles to the press. Thus, either orientation could result without thought.

"When examining the actual stamp and later on studying pictures of the stamp, it became apparent that the printing lines were much sharper and clearer on the horizontal example than on the vertical stamps. This then, leads one to the conclusion that the single horizontal laid paper variety was produced from the die and not the plate."

Collectors believe no more than 10 stamps of the vertically laid stamps were produced; possibly, only a block of six was printed.

The horizontally laid stamp can be traced back to the Ferrari sales in 1922. During the same sales, a vertically laid copy was sold. Alfred Lichtenstein bought both of these. They were later sold by H.R. Harmer as part of the Dale-Lichtenstein collection.

According to Pratt, a second copy of the vertically laid paper stamp was bought at ANPHILEX, and a third copy was exhibited at the show. He said another copy is in a collection in England.

Two copies, from the King Carol of Romania collection, were exhibited at the INTERPHIL international stamp show in Philadelphia in 1976.

A copy of the 1/- on vertically laid paper was part of the Pratt collection sold by Harmers of London October 21, 1986. It realized £5,500 (about $8,000), including the 10-percent buyer's premium.

Christie's also auctioned a copy on vertically laid paper during its October 30, 1986, Isleham collection sale. The stamp — the ex-Ferrari, Dale-Liechtenstein copy — realized $13,750, including the 10-percent buyer's premium.

The Scott catalog lists the laid-paper copies of the 1/- orange at $20,000 mint. No used copies exist.

Only Half Right

VALUE: $6,000
The overprint was omitted on the left stamp of this pair of 1929 3-penny airmail stamps issued by Papua.

Among the scarce airmail stamps in the world is an error from the Pacific island of Papua New Guinea. Great Britain established the eastern half of New Guinea as a protectorate in 1884. The protectorate was called, appropriately, British New Guinea. In 1905, administration of British New Guinea was transferred to Australia, and in 1906, the territory was renamed Papua.

The first stamps bearing the name "Papua" appeared in 1907. These featured the lakatoi, a sailing vessel of the island. This design also had been used for the first stamps of British New Guinea.

When, in 1929, the Papua Post Office recognized a need for airmail stamps, postal officials ordered the overprinting of this first Papuan issue to designate their use on airmail. The airmail stamps were to be used primarily on mail to be carried over Australian routes. The Lakatoi stamps were overprinted locally. Three printings exist of the original Lakatoi issue, and all three were overprinted "AIR MAIL" in black.

The Harrison printing is on yellowish toned or colored paper with sepia centers. The Cooke printings are on similar paper but with black or gray-black centers. The Ash printings are on white paper with dark gray or black centers.

The overprint cliches were set up in a block of 10 (5 by 2) and applied four times to the sheets of Lakatoi stamps from the three printings. Later, the overprint was applied by a setting in a 5-by-8 format to the Ash printing only.

The local printer erred in overprinting the sheets. Stamps exist on the Cooke and Ash printings with the overprint omitted. This was first discovered in 1929 when London stamp dealer R. Roberts received his shipment of new issues from Papua. Upon opening his supply of the new Papuan overprints, he discovered that some of the stamps on one sheet were missing the overprint.

Roberts broke up the sheet into strips featuring the normal overprinted stamps with the missing-overprint varieties.

Only 10 vertical pairs of the Cooke printing exist showing the normal overprint on one stamp and the missing-overprint variety on the other. The Ash printing also is known with the overprint omitted in vertical and horizontal pairs.

The Scott catalog does not distinguish between printings. It lists the vertical pairs as C1b and prices them at $4,250. Horizontal pairs are listed as C1c and priced at $6,000. Only mint examples exist. A vertical pair with the missing-overprint variety was sold by Greg Manning Auctions at its October 30-November 1, 1987, sale. It realized $3,080, including a 10-percent buyer's premium.

PHILIPPINES

Straight-Pin Varieties

VALUE: $4,500

A stamp-shortage emergency in the Philippines during World War II caused the release of crudely overprinted stamps in 1944. This 1-peso "Victory" provisional is one of the islands' greatest philatelic rarities.

General Douglas MacArthur fulfilled his promise and returned to liberate the Philippines in 1944. Nineteen days after the first American troops landed on Leyte, provisional stamps overprinted "VICTORY" made their debut.

The basic stamps used for the overprinting were pre-war issues inscribed "United States of America/Commonwealth of the Philippines." Most of these stamps were stained and worn.

Following their invasion of the islands, the Japanese confiscated supplies of Philippines stamps. When the Americans landed on the Philippines, most of the islands were still in enemy hands as were the stocks of stamps.

As villages were liberated, the supplies of stamps slowly were recovered. Some were found in chests; others had been buried to hide them from the captors. When they were recovered, the stamps were sent to Tacloban to be handstamped "VICTORY." The crude rubber handstamp used for the overprinting deteriorated rapidly. It finally broke in half and had to be pinned together with a straight pin. This resulted in many varieties on the provisionals.

The islands suffered from a severe shortage of stamps. Postmasters were under strict orders not to sell stamps for philatelic purposes. At many post offices, the only way to obtain stamps was to present the letter to be mailed. The postal clerk affixed the stamp to the letter and placed the letter into the mailstream.

The shortage of basic stamps accounts for the scarcity of these provisional issues. Only when more adequate supplies of stamps became available through the liberation of the islands were collectors allowed to purchase stamps for their collections. Even then they usually were limited to one set, or occasionally blocks of four of the provisional stamps.

In the May 1954 *Collectors Club Philatelist*, Idus L. Murphree told of his experiences with the emergency issue. Murphree was stationed on a battleship that was patrolling the entrance to Leyte Gulf. He was a stamp collector, as were other members of the crew. When he was ordered to go ashore to pick up intelligence charts from the Army, he could not resist stopping at the post office to buy stamps.

He asked the postal clerk for a sheet of everything on sale at the post office. The shocked clerk wasted no time in explaining the situation to Murphree. Because of the shortage, stamps were sacred in the Philippines. It was impossible to buy sheets. The clerk agreed to sell Murphree two stamps — one for Murphree and one for Murphree's buddy who had accompanied him ashore.

Some of the "Victory" provisionals were issued in quantities fewer than 50. Only 21 copies of the 1 peso were overprinted. In the *Possessions* journal for the first quarter of 1982, Gilbert N. Plass said only 10 copies of this stamp have been recorded.

This is by far the most expensive of the provisionals. The Scott catalog lists it at $7,000 mint and $4,500 used. Harmers of New York sold an example of this rarity at its June 25-26, 1986, auction for $1,870, including the 10-percent buyer's premium.

Plass notes that another value of this set is much scarcer than the 1p. Only three copies have been recorded of the 2-centavo Rizal, known as Scott 463B. Scott lists it at $1,450 mint and used.

Some postal cards and stamped envelopes bearing the "VICTORY" overprint also are scarce. Plass records only seven copies of the 4¢ carmine on white envelope. Five copies have been recorded of the 2¢ red on pale buff postal card.

PORTUGUESE GUINEA

Cliche of Another Country

VALUE: $6,325

A pair of the Portuguese Guinea 1881 overprint. The left stamp is the normal Cape Verde issue; the right is the misplaced Mozambique cliche.

Was Cape Verde's cliche error intentionally created? This question has been asked by many collectors. In the late 1800s, the Portuguese Post Office issued a series of typographed stamps for the Portuguese colonies. Each set featured a common design — a crown — with the name of the individual colony inserted. (Portuguese India was the exception; it began issuing stamps with its own designs in 1871.)

In 1877, the Portuguese Post Office released a set of these Crown stamps for Cape Verde, a group of islands in the Atlantic, off the coast of Africa. During the printing of these stamps at the Lisbon Mint, the printer inserted a cliche of the Mozambique 40-reis Crown stamp into a plate of the Cape Verde issue of the same denomination.

Pairs of stamps were discovered with one stamp carrying the "CABO VERDE" inscription and printed se-tenant with another carrying a "MOCAMBIQUE" inscription. The philatelic press reported this error shortly after the 40r blue stamp was issued.

The 40r blue error exists perforated 12½ or 13½. Scott catalog lists the perf 12½ stamp at $1,000 mint and $900 used, and the perf 13½ at $1,750 mint and used.

VALUE: $12,650

The Cape Verde cliche error overprinted for Portuguese Guinea franks this cover, along with a single of the normal issue and two 1885 10r.

Discovery of the error delighted collectors, and prices rose accordingly. However, the discovery of a similar error on the 40r yellow buff stamp in 1881 aroused collectors' suspicion.

By 1881, the Cape Verde Post Office and the Lisbon Mint were aware of the 1877 error. In *Crown Stamps of the Portuguese Colonies*, Rufino R. Pernes refers to an article in the 1892 *Annual Stamp News*. In the article, J.N. Marsden, a Lisbon collector who was noted for his expertise in Portugal and Portuguese colonies, reported on his visit to Cape Verde in 1884 where he purchased sheets of the 40r blue and 40r yellow buff from which the error had been cut out. Marsden said he had been assured that the sheets had been received from Lisbon in that condition. Nearly ten years later, he purchased a sheet of the 40r yellow buff with the error intact. The error was still on sale at Cape Verde post offices.

Pernes, like other collectors, believes the 1881 error was intentional. Otherwise, he says, the cliche of the Mozambique stamp would have been removed. The 1881 error exists perf 12½ and imperforate. Although the 40r imperf stamps were not intended to be used for postage, they were sold at post offices in Cape Verde.

The prices of the 1881 error reflect collectors' suspicions. Scott catalog lists the perf 12½ stamps at $85 mint and used. The imperf variety of the error is known only in mint condition and is listed in Scott at $27.50.

Pernes says the perf 13½ errors of 1877 are the scarcest of the Cape Verde issues, since they were printed in a smaller quantity. Of even greater rarity is the error cliche overprinted for use in Portuguese Guinea. Cape Verde stamps were overprinted "GUINE" beginning in 1881 for use in Portuguese Guinea. The first overprints consisted of small capital letters in black. This overprint on the cliche error is extremely scarce. Scott catalog lists it at $5,500 mint and $5,250 used.

On May 30, 1986, at the AMERIPEX international stamp show in Chicago, David Feldman auctioned a pair consisting of the overprinted error and the normal overprinted Cape Verde 40r. It realized $6,325, including a 15-percent buyer's premium. At the same sale, Feldman auctioned a cover franked with four of the Portuguese Guinea overprints, one being the misplaced 40r cliche. It sold for $12,650, including a 15-percent buyer's premium.

A larger "GUINE" overprint was used in red or black from 1881 to 1885. The 40r blue misplaced cliche with this overprint is listed in Scott at $900 mint and $750 used. Once again, prices reflect the unpopularity of the 40r yellow buff cliche error. With the "GUINE" overprint, this stamp is listed by Scott at $30 mint and $27.50 used.

RHODESIA

Disappearing Perfs

VALUE: $16,000

Only five examples of this Rhodesia 1905 1/- Victoria Falls error exist. The pair is missing the horizontal perforations, and it is known as a vertical pair imperforate between.

Two rare perforation varieties exist on the 1905 1/- Victoria Falls issue from Rhodesia. Pairs exist imperforate and imperf between.

Rhodesia's stamps bore the name British South Africa Company until 1924 when the area was divided into Northern Rhodesia and Southern Rhodesia under direct British rule. The name Rhodesia was added to the British South Africa Company stamps in 1909. The British South Africa Company named the territory Rhodesia in 1895 in honor of Cecil John Rhodes, whose ambition was to extend British domination through the central territories of Africa. Rhodes urged the incorporation of mercantile company, British South Africa Company, in 1889 under royal charter. His objective was to acquire commercial and administrative rights over these territories. Although Rhodesia was named for Rhodes in 1895, the stamps did not reflect this until 1909.

In 1905, the British South Africa Company issued a set of stamps to mark the visit of the British Association to Rhodesia and the opening of the Victoria Falls Bridge across the Zambezi River. The set consisted of six values — 1 penny, 2½d, 5d, 1/-, 2/6d and 5/-. Each shows a view of Victoria Falls reproduced from a photograph in the London offices of the British South Africa Company. The stamps feature an engine-turned border. The inscription "BRITISH SOUTH AFRICA/ COMPANY" appears in two lines at the top with "VICTORIA FALLS" at the bottom. The date "1905" appears in the upper corners; the denomination in the lower corners.

Waterlow and Sons printed the stamps by intaglio process in sheets of 25 (five rows of five stamps).

Major errors occurred during the printing of the 1/- value. One sheet contained five pairs of stamps with the horizontal perforations missing. These are known as vertical pairs imperf between. Another sheet had all vertical perforations missing except on the margins. Pairs from this sheet are horizontal pairs imperf between. Imperforate pairs also exist. These have no perforations at all.

The catalog values reflect the scarcity of these errors. The Scott catalog lists the imperf-between pairs at $16,000. The imperforate pairs catalog at $18,500. These errors seldom come on the market, as is indicated by their italicized price in Scott.

Farouk's Inverted Eagle

VALUE: $12,500

The only known multiple of Russia's 1902-05 7-ruble stamp with the center inverted. The marginal block of four was once owned by King Farouk.

    Errors and varieties frequently occurred on Russia's Arms stamp series. Although many of these are common, a few are rarities.

    Inverted-center errors excite collectors, and the Russian Arms series offers several of these errors. A one-of-a-kind multiple of one of these inverts rates as one of the world's great philatelic rarities.

    Russia introduced the Arms series as the first postage stamps of the Russian Empire in 1857. This design continued in use until after the revolution of 1917. Some values were drawn back into service in the early 1920s when high inflation brought about the need to surcharge these issues.

    The Arms design features the doubled-headed imperial eagle with the scepter in one claw and the orb in the other. The eagle is surmounted by the imperial crown. The Imperial State Printing Office produced these stamps in two or three passes through the press. The inverted centers occurred when sheets bearing the

103

printed frames were fed into the press upside down.

Some of these inverts are relatively common, cataloging at $300 or less. One screaming rarity, however, is the 7-kopeck of the 1875-79 series with the center inverted. Known only in used condition, it catalogs at $17,500.

Many of the inverted centers in the Arms series exist used. This is understandable because at first glance it is difficult to tell that the eagle is upside down.

The rare multiple mentioned previously is a marginal block of four of the 7-ruble stamp of the 1902-05 series. This is the only multiple known to exist of this 7rub invert. Egypt's King Farouk owned this block of four, along with numerous other rarities. Following the death of Farouk, Robert W. Baughman bought the block to add to his fabulous collection of Imperial Russia.

When Robert A. Siegel Auction Galleries sold Baughman's collection during four auctions March 24-27, 1971, the block realized $3,600. The winning bidder was Norman D. Epstein. Harmers of New York sold Epstein's collection October 15-16, 1985. Included among the Russian rarities was the block of the 7rub invert. It realized $12,500, including the 10-percent buyer's premium.

The Scott catalog lists single copies of the 7rub invert at $5,000 mint and used.

Where's The Surcharge?

VALUE: $7,700

The surcharge is omitted on the bottom stamp of this pair of the St. Helena 1-shilling-on-6-penny stamp.

St. Helena adopted an unusual method of printing stamps and in the process created several rarities. This tiny South Atlantic island, most famous as Napoleon's asylum when he was exiled from France, issued its first stamp in 1856. St. Helena, a poor island, could not afford to squander its money on elaborately produced postage stamps. So its postal officials devised a cost-efficient, yet attractive stamp that would meet its needs.

In January 1856, St. Helena issued a 6-penny stamp portraying Queen Victoria. Perkins, Bacon and Company of England prepared a lovely die, engraved by William Humphrys, from which this stamp was produced.

In fact, all St. Helena stamps were produced from this die until 1890. Whenever a new value was required, the postal officials simply ordered a new surcharge to be applied to the 6d stamp.

In 1863, Perkins, Bacon lost the contract to print the 6d stamps, and the plates were transferred to De La Rue, also of England, who printed the stamp for the remainder of its life.

Postal rates also were revised in 1863, making new denominations of stamps necessary. The ever-prudent postal officials ordered De La Rue to print the 6d stamps in various colors and then surcharge them with the appropriate values. The first set of these surcharged issues was imperforate. Beginning in 1864, the stamps were perforated.

St. Helena's unusual method of printing stamps led to the creation of many errors and varieties. Collectors have discovered double surcharges and missing surcharges. The surcharge errors occurred when the sheet was misplaced on the surcharging press, producing a row of double-surcharged stamps and a row of stamps with the surcharge omitted.

Among the rarities of these St. Helena surcharges are the double surcharges on the 1d on 6d brown-red (surcharge 17 millimeters) and 4d on 6d carmine of 1863, and the 4d on 6d carmine of the 1864-73 series. Double surcharges also occur on the 1d on 6d brown-red, 3d on 6d dark violet, 4d on 6d carmine, and 1 shilling on 6d yellow-green of the 1868 series. This error is again found on the ½d on 6d green and 3d on 6d deep violet of the 1884-94 series, the 2½d on 6d blue of 1893, and the 1/- on 6d yellow green of 1894. The Scott catalog prices these double surcharges from $1,500 to $16,500.

Among the most spectacular of the errors of these surcharged issues are the imperforate pairs of the 1868 series and the missing surcharges on the 4d on 6d carmine of the 1863 series, and the 4d on 6d carmine and the 1/- on 6d yellow-green of the 1868 series.

Particularly interesting are the copies with the surcharge omitted.

When separated from stamps bearing the surcharges, these stamps appear to be errors of color rather than missing-surcharge errors. The Scott catalog prices the 1863 4d on 6d with surcharge omitted at $14,000. The 4d on 6d carmine of 1868 with surcharge omitted is noted by Scott but is not priced or numbered. The pair of the 1/- on 6d yellow green of 1868, with one stamp missing the surcharge, is priced at $15,000.

An example of this pair realized $7,700, including a 10-percent buyer's premium, at the March 11, 1987, Isleham collection auction conducted by Christie's in New York City. This pair was once in the collection of pharmaceutical magnate Josiah K. Lilly.

A Steamship Local

VALUE: $2,300
A blue framed example of the St. Lucia Steam Conveyance local stamp.

From St. Lucia, one of the poorest islands in the West Indies, comes one of the rarest local stamps in the world.

In 1869, the St. Lucia Steam Conveyance Company Ltd. was established to carry passengers, freight and mail between the capital of Castries and the towns on the west coast of the island. There were no roads running between these towns. Today, St. Lucia still has few paved roads.

The St. Lucia Steam Conveyance Company issued its first local stamp in 1870 — a crude gummed label. This stamp was to be applied to mail carried on the steamer *Aide*. The stamp paid postage equal to 1 penny.

The first issue is an unframed gummed label bearing part of the company's rubber stamp. The rubber stamp shows the name "*St. Lucia Steam Conveyance*," in a double circle. Later St. Lucia Steam Conveyance stamps feature the rubber-stamped impression on top of a blue frame. These locals are most distinguishable by the large manuscript cross that cancels each of them.

The St. Lucia locals are extremely scarce. Only six have been recorded. Tragically, the one copy found on an entire was lost in the mail in 1972. L.N. Williams, noted writer, cinderella specialist and *Linn's* Locals of the World columnist, told the fate of this item.

Williams' brother, the late Maurice Williams, also was a cinderella specialist and philatelic author. After examining the cover bearing the St. Lucia stamp, Maurice sent it by registered mail to its owner with a certificate of authenticity from the Philatelic Information Bureau. The registered envelope carrying the rarity never arrived.

The entire was addressed to "Messieurs Macfarlane & Moffat & Co., Negts a Castries." L.N. Williams says the stamp was affixed to the top left corner of the cover and canceled by the manuscript cross. The unframed stamp is on piece. Williams says the piece bears a small part of the same address that was on the entire.

When the Cartier collection was auctioned September 15, 1977, a copy of the St. Lucia local realized £2,100 (about $3,700). This stamp was sold by Stanley Gibbons at its September 4-7, 1979, auction for £2,420 ($5,800), the highest price ever realized for a St. Lucia Stamp Conveyance local.

David Feldman SA sold two examples of these stamps, including the unframed issue, at its November 19-23, 1985, auction in New York City. The unframed example realized only $920, including a 15-percent buyer's premium. A framed version sold for $2,300, including the 15-percent buyer's premium.

Check The Perfs

VALUE: $15,000
St. Vincent's 6-penny yellow-green of 1861 is scarce in mint condition.

Two of the most strikingly beautiful stamps of the British West Indies are the first stamps of St. Vincent. This first issue also is one of St. Vincent's greatest rarities, particularly the 6-penny denomination. In 1860, Bouverie Alleyne, St. Vincent's colonial secretary, wrote to the British printer Perkins, Bacon & Company and asked the printer to prepare stamps similar to Great Britain's Penny Black, with the name St. Vincent added. Perkins, Bacon could not comply with this request. The company did offer to print stamps for the island but insisted that they differ from those of Great Britain.

The St. Vincent officials agreed. The new stamps featured a portrait of Queen Victoria by Edward Henry Corbould. Charles Henry Jeens engraved the issue. The 1d stamp was printed in rose; the 6d in yellow green. The book *St. Vincent* by A.D. Pierce, J.L. Messenger and Robson Lowe points out that the first-issue 1d frequently is confused with the 1d of the 1862-66 series because of similarities in color and perforations. The Scott catalog says the first issue can be distinguished from the second by the perforations. The first issue features clean-cut perfs; the second issue shows rough perfs.

But the authors of the *St. Vincent* book say the perfs on the first issue vary from partly clean cut to partly rough. This makes the stamp difficult to distinguish from the second issue.

Some collectors prefer to collect this stamp on cover, where the date of the postmark can help to attest to the earlier release.

Mint copies of the 1d first issue are much scarcer than used copies. The Scott catalog prices mint copies at $12,500 and used at $1,250. By comparison, the second-issue 1d catalogs at $47.50

VALUE: $12,500
A mint example of the striking 1861
1-penny rose stamp from St. Vincent.

mint and $25 used. Covers bearing the first issue are scarce. The *St. Vincent* book refers to five recorded covers. One, formerly in the Eugene Klein and Lickfold collections, bears a strip of four and a single with the St. Vincent datestamp of September 20, 1861. This cover was sold by Harmers of New York in its November 23, 1964, auction.

Another cover, bearing a strip of four of the 1d and a horizontal pair of the 6d, was sold as part of the April 25-27, 1950, Schenck sale by Harmer, Rooke of New York. It carries a datestamp of August 24, 1861.

Robson Lowe sold a St. Vincent first-issue cover in a June 28, 1950, auction. It bears a strip of four of the 1d and a vertical pair of the 6d with the datestamp of February 8, 1862.

The *St. Vincent* book also mentions a large piece bearing a strip of three, a pair and a single, with a datestamp of June 28, 1862.

The fifth item mentioned in the book is a strip of five on a wrapper dated December 1861. This was auctioned as part of the Charlton Henry sale by Harmer, Rooke of New York on April 6, 1961.

Imperforate varieties exist of the 1d. These possibly crept out of the printers' facilities as printer's waste. No used examples have been recorded. The Scott catalog lists this variety at $750.

The scarcer of the two first-issue values is the 6d. It can be distinguished from the second-issue 6d by its distinctive yellow-green color. The second issue is dark green. Mint copies are exceptionally rare. The Scott catalog lists these at $15,000. Used copies catalog at $600. A mint pair was in the Lichfield collection.

A Scarce Provisional

VALUE: Indeterminable

The largest multiple of the St. Vincent 4-penny on 1/- provisional of 1881 is this strip of three in the Royal Collection in Buckingham Palace.

St. Vincent's scarcest stamp, although it may not be its most expensive, is a provisional issued in 1881.

Beginning in 1880, this island in the West Indies surcharged contemporary stamps with new values for provisional use. The 1/- vermilion was surcharged "4d" (4 pence) in black with a bar below the denomination.

Only 21 sheets (630 stamps) were surcharged with the new value. Few have survived.

The Scott catalog lists mint copies of this provisional at $3,000 and used at $1,500. Multiples of the 4d on 1/- are extremely scarce and are likely to bring far in excess of the catalog value when sold.

The largest multiple, however, is unlikely to ever come on the market again. It is a mint strip of three, now in the Royal Collection in Buckingham Palace. This strip was once in the collection of the Earl of Crawford. Another stunning item is a first-day cover. This cover is addressed to "Mr. G. Lindsay/Wesleyan Chapel/St. John's Square/E.C." The provisional is tied by the "K" cancellation used in Kingston. The cover also bears a circular datestamp, "St.-Vincent/A/NO 28/81." In the upper left-hand corner is a manuscript "England." Also on the left-hand side is a London "PAID"

VALUE: Indeterminable

The only known first-day cover of the 4-penny on 1/- provisional stamp is addressed to G. Lindsay, Wesleyan Chapel, St. John's Square, E.C. The rare 1881 provisional surcharge is tied by a Kingston "K" cancellation.

circular datestamp.

John F. Seybold bought the first-day cover from M. Giewelb for £20. Major Charlton Henry later purchased the cover. It was sold when the Henry collection was auctioned by Harmer, Rooke and Company in New York in 1961.

Collectors are cautioned that this provisional has been faked both on and off cover. All copies should be expertized.

SERBIA

A Collector's Favor?

VALUE: $39,100

The only recorded example of Serbia's 1872-79 1-para tete-beche pair.

A tete-beche pair from Serbia has been the subject of much speculation among stamp collectors. Only one such pair has been recorded, leading some collectors to question whether the pair was legitimately issued.

Serbia was once an independent kingdom in southeastern Europe. Following World War I, Serbia united with Montenegro, Bosnia and Herzegovina, Croatia, Dalmatia and Slovenia to form the kingdom that later became the Republic of Yugoslavia.

Serbia issued its first stamps in 1866. These feature the coat of arms or the portrait of Prince Michael.

When Prince Milan acceded to the throne, Serbia issued a new set of stamps portraying the prince. These stamps were printed in Belgrade. The 1869-78 series portraying Prince Milan was perforated 9½, 12 and with compound perforations. The 1872-79 series was imperforate. The 1-para yellow tete-beche pair comes from this series of imperf stamps. In a tete-beche pair, one stamp is upside down.

Little is known about this one-of-a-kind pair. It first appeared in the collection of Count Ferrari, the Frenchman who strove to acquire every stamp issued in the world. Ferrari owned one of the most fabulous collections of stamps ever formed.

Was the tete-beche pair an error or was it deliberately produced? Collectors may never know.

Collector Paul Zhivotich wrote about Serbia's early issues in the February 1975 issue of *The London Philatelist*, the journal of the Royal Philatelic Society of London. Zhivotich speculated that the tete-beche pair was produced at the request of Ferrari. He says Ferrari visited Belgrade in the mid-1890s and entertained Belgrade dignitaries on his yacht. Zhivotich suggests that the tete-beche pair was printed especially for Ferrari, since the dignitaries knew their foreign visitor's love for stamps.

Despite speculation such as this, collectors regard this tete-beche pair as one of the great rarities of eastern Europe. Most major catalogs recognize the pair as a legitimate variety. The Scott catalog lists it as Serbia 25a but gives no price because of the infrequency of sales of this item. David Feldman SA sold this rarity at its AMERIPEX auction on May 30, 1986. The pair realized $39,100, including a 15-percent buyer's premium.

Escaped The Fires

VALUE: $4,620

This 1855 1/- violet from South Australia was never released because its color too closely resembled that of the 6-penny blue. Most examples of the 1/- stamps were destroyed.

Only a few copies of the South Australia 1/- violet Victoria stamp of 1855 escaped the fires when the entire stock of stamps was ordered destroyed. Today, these stamps realize thousands of dollars when they are sold.

The British colony of South Australia issued its own stamps from 1855 until it was united with five other British colonies in 1901 to form the Commonwealth of Australia.

The British printing firm of Perkins, Bacon & Company produced South Australia's first issue, a set of four values portraying Queen Victoria facing left. Postal authorities were disturbed, however, when the stamps arrived from England. They discovered that the colors of the 6-penny blue and 1/- violet were so similar that they were barely distinguishable. Introducing the use of postage stamps to the colony was difficult enough without adding to the confusion by releasing stamps of different values with similar colors.

John Watts, South Australia's postmaster general, ordered the entire 500,000 1/- stamps destroyed. His order was carried out June 5, 1857. A notice from the South Australia Treasury Department states, "We hereby certify that we have this day burnt and destroyed 2083 80/240 sheets: — 500,000 shilling postage stamps in accordance with the instructions contained in the Honourable the Chief Secretary's letter of the 24th ult., No. 664/57 addressed to the Postmaster General."

But collectors today know that not all the 1/- violet stamps were destroyed. A few escaped the fires.

When these stamps first came on the market, collectors were puzzled by their existence. None are known used, so collectors assumed the stamps were proofs.

However, a search of the archives in Adelaide by a group of collectors turned up correspondence between the postmaster general, the printer and the treasurer revealing that the stamps were intended for issue but were destroyed.

The Scott catalog lists the 1/- violet at $10,000. Christie's of New York sold a copy at its March 11, 1987, Isleham sale for $4,620, including a 10-percent buyer's premium.

John Griffiths, a well-known collector, owns a copy of the 1/- violet. Griffiths exhibited the stamp in the court of honor at the Hafnia international stamp show in Denmark.

The Royal Collection in Buckingham Palace has a copy as does the Tapling collection at the British Library.

An example of the stamp owned by Lieutenant Colonel Harry Napier was sold by Robson Lowe in the 1970s.

John Boker, who is best known for his collection of German States, which has brought record prices at auction, sold a copy of the South Australian stamp.

Griffiths said six copies exist with a bar cancel with the word "CANCEL" written in the center. He said these copies originally were in a block of six that was cut into singles. The cancels were prepared by Perkins, Bacon, thus leaving collectors to believe that unused copies of the stamp came from the same source.

A canceled copy is in the Royal Collection. Griffiths and Peter Jaffe of Australia also own canceled copies.

An 'N' For An 'H'

VALUE: $5,500
One of four used copies of the South Australia 1903 "EIGNT" error.

South Australia packed more rarities into its short stamp-issuing history than perhaps any other country. Its most famous, of course, is the 1879 4-penny ultramarine with missing surcharge. Another is the 1855-56 1/- violet.

One of the most interesting of the South Australia rarities features a spelling error. This error occurred on the 8-penny value of the 1902-03 series, known as the Long stamps.

The Long stamps were produced in two separate processes. The central portion of the stamp, including the portrait of Queen Victoria surrounded by "SOUTH AUSTRALIA," was printed from a plate produced by Thomas De La Rue of England. The stamp also features a tablet at the top with the word "POSTAGE" and one at the bottom for the value. These were added later.

When the post office of South Australia required a new printing of the stamps, the loose forms containing the words "POSTAGE" and the values were inserted in place, and the stamps were printed. This eliminated the need for more than one plate for the design.

Several varieties in the "POSTAGE" and value tablets occurred. The most notable and scarcest occurred on the 8d. A few examples of this stamp exist with the value misspelled "EIGNT."

A local printer in South Australia produced the "POSTAGE" and value tablets. The spelling error occurred when one of the workers attempted to correct a broken letter.

The late J.R.W. Purves, one of the great collectors of Australia, once quoted a reference to the error in the *Australian Philatelist* for September 1904. The article reported, "We also hear that they have had to employ a local firm to prepare their stereos. This is how the error 'EIGNT' originated."

The February 1912 *Australian Philatelist* featured an interview with the printer, J.B. Cooke. In the interview, Cooke said a typeset form impression was taken in wax, but that in the making of one of these for the "EIGHT PENCE" value plate, the "H" stuck to the wax. He said the compositor mistakenly replaced it with an "N," "for which mistake he was dismissed."

Purves pointed out that this statement was "not wholly satisfactory," since it was made eight years after the error occurred.

The "EIGNT" error is surely the most striking of the South Australian rarities. Only 60 of these errors were produced. Few survive. Used copies are extremely scarce. Only four have been recorded.

Colonial Stamp Company in Los Angeles sold one of the used copies in its September 30, 1987, auction. It realized $5,500. The Scott catalog lists the error at $2,000 mint, $2,750 used.

SOUTH GEORGIA

Seeing Double

VALUE: $2,000

One of two examples of the double surcharge on the Falklands 1928 2½-penny provisional appears on the upper left stamp of this block of four.

The arrival of a whaling fleet at the barren, mountainous island of South Georgia created such a demand for stamps that it required the printing of a provisional issue to meet this demand.

South Georgia is a dependency of the Falkland Islands, a group

121

of islands located about 300 miles east of the Straits of Magellan at the southern end of South America.

Although in recent years South Georgia has issued its own stamps, as well as using those of the Falkland Island Dependencies, until 1944 it used the stamps of the Falkland Islands.

In 1928, the whaling fleet and the *RRS William Scoresby* arrived at South Georgia. The crew used most of the ½-penny and 2½d Falkland stamps available at Grytviken Post Office.

To prevent his stock from being totally exhausted, the postmaster ordered the creation of a provisional stamp. He surcharged the contemporary Falkland Islands 2d George V stamps with a new value, "2½D," in black. Salvesen's Whaling Station at Leith Harbour produced the brass die used for the surcharge. When new supplies of stamps arrived on the island, this die was defaced.

A total of 1,179 provisionals were on sale at Grytviken Post Office for two weeks. Most of these have since been lost or destroyed.

Today, the stamp is a rarity. The Scott catalog prices the provisional at $1,750 mint and $2,000 used.

An extremely scarce variety is the South Georgia provisional showing a double surcharge. Only two copies have been recorded. David Feldman SA sold an example of this variety at its November 10-14, 1986, auction. The double surcharge appears in the upper left stamp in a block of four.

The other copy, also in a block of four, was sold by Harmers of London on October 2, 1979, for £21,000. The double overprint in this block is in the upper right. This block later changed hands for the reported price of 57,500 Swiss francs.

It's No Gimmick

VALUE: $6,000
A manuscript black "2" surcharge appears on the 1867 1½¢-on-½-anna stamp of Straits Settlements.

A curious issue from Straits Settlements is a manuscript "2" surcharge on the already-surcharged 1½¢-on-½-anna stamp.

The British colony of Straits Settlements, located on the Malay Peninsula in southeast Asia, began issuing stamps September 1, 1867. This set consists of Indian stamps surcharged with new values in red, blue, black, violet or green. A small crown also is part of the surcharge. While the original Indian stamps bear denominations in annas, the Straits Settlements' surcharges are in cents.

A few years after the release of this set, collectors discovered a copy of the 1½¢-on-½a stamp with a manuscript "2" over the surcharge and with a pen mark obliterating the "THREE HALF" surcharge. Collectors' first reaction was to discard the manuscript surcharge as a philatelic gimmick.

In reporting the discovery to his readers, the editor of the *Philatelic Journal* in 1872 said the surcharge was done by someone who had nothing better to do. In other words, the manuscript surcharge had no validity. A few years later, however, copies of the manuscript-surcharged stamp turned up genuinely used on covers from the island of Penang.

Major E.B. Evans wrote in the *Philatelist* in September 1876 that he had seen a copy of this stamp that had done duty as 2¢.

Genuinely used copies began appearing on the market more frequently. Today, used copies are more common than the mint stamps. The Scott catalog lists mint copies at $7,500; used at $6,000. Bacon noted that all genuine specimens he had seen were postmarked with the "D17" cancel of Penang.

The question remained: Why was this stamp issued?

In his study of the Straits Settlements, the late Dr. F.E. Wood said he believed the stamps were issued in 1869 to fulfill a need for 2¢ stamps in Penang. He pointed out that the Penang Treasury report for that year showed there were only 640 2¢ stamps remaining on the island on January 2, 1869. He said that although this number had increased to 6,720 by April 1, it was likely there had been a shortage of stamps during the first quarter of 1869. This led to the creation of the manuscript provisionals.

Wood speculated that the manuscript stamps were sold over the post office counter, as well as through stamp vendors, since some of the genuine copies carry a business firm's chop marks in addition to the postmark. The post office probably chose the 1½¢-on-½a stamps for surcharging because there was little need for the 1½¢ denomination. This belief is supported because no 1½¢ stamps were included in the permanent set of 1867-72.

Although collectors doubted the legitimacy of the manuscript provisional at first, it has become one of the most important issues of the Straits Settlements.

Stop The Presses

VALUE: $11,000
Only a few examples of the 1899 5¢ of the Straits Settlements exist without the "FOUR CENTS" surcharge.

A fluctuation in currency led to the creation of one of the Straits Settlements' scarcest stamps. The Straits Settlements was a British colony in Malaya, comprising Singapore, Penang, Province Wellesley and Malacca, along with the Cocos (Keeling) Islands, Christmas Island and Labuan. Japan occupied the Straits Settlements during World War II. The colony was dissolved in 1946.

When the Straits Settlements adopted the Imperial Penny Postage in 1898, the postal authorities set the imperial postal rate at 5¢. Crown Agents, which represented the Straits Settlements, sent a request for 5¢ stamps to the printer, Thomas De La Rue, in England. The stamps were to be printed in red.

The request confused De La Rue because it already was printing the Straits Settlements 3¢ denomination in red. The two stamps featured the same design, a portrait of Queen Victoria facing left.

According to John Easton's *The De La Rue History of British &*

Foreign Postage Stamps, the printer questioned Crown Agents about the decision to print another red stamp. Crown Agents agreed to send a telegram to the colony asking for an explanation. In the meantime, it asked De La Rue to suspend printing of both the 3¢ and 5¢ stamps. De La Rue agreed to stop printing the 3¢ but explained that the 5¢ already had been printed in red.

Crown Agents received a telegram from the Straits Settlements stating that "the Five Cents stamp will become the equivalent of the penny and should be printed in red, and the colour of the Three Cents should be changed, preferably to brown."

Easton said De La Rue already had printed 36,000 5¢ in brown and decided to print 216,000 in red. On November 9, 1898, the printer received another request for 1,235,000 5¢ stamps in red.

The Straits Settlements' currency was on the silver standard in 1898; therefore, the value of the dollar varied with the price of silver. In his study of the Straits Settlements, the late Dr. F.E. Wood said the average value of the dollar in 1898 no longer justified a rate of 5¢ as the equivalent of 1 penny. The postal authorities decided that the new stamp should be 4¢, not 5¢.

Since the 5¢ red stamps already had been printed, Crown Agents asked De La Rue to surcharge these with "FOUR CENTS." At the same time, the 5¢ ultramarine, 5¢ brown and 8¢ ultramarine stamps were surcharged "4/cents" in two lines. The surcharged stamps were released in March 1899.

A few mint copies of the 5¢ red exist without the surcharge. The Scott catalog lists these at $11,000.

Sir Edward Denny Bacon, who was keeper of the Royal Collection from 1913 until his death in 1938, said the Straits Settlements missing-surcharge stamps are not errors. He said they are proofs. According to Bacon, "The few specimens that are known, four or five at the most, have all come from official sources in London, and there can be no doubt that no specimens without the surcharge were ever sent out to the colony."

A Questionable Issue

VALUE: $2,500
The Sweden 1891 5-ore brown — is it an error of color or a proof?

A proof or a color error? This is the question collectors of Sweden have asked for years about the 5-ore brown of 1891. Although many collectors today lean heavily toward the opinion that the stamp is a proof, most of the major stamp catalogs, including Scott and Michel, list it as an error of color. Regardless of its status, the stamp is a great rarity. Only nine exist.

In 1891, the Swedish Post Office introduced a set of stamps. The 1o through 4o values feature an ornamental design with the denomination expressed as a numeral in the center. The 5o through 50o stamps portray King Oscar II. The 1-krona value carries a similar portrait, but with a different frame.

As Sweden's first engraved stamps, the 5o through 1kr values set the pace for years to come. Today, Sweden's engraved issues are among the finest in the world. It all began with the exquisitely engraved Oscar II issues. These stamps were engraved by Max Mirowsky and printed by Jacob Bagge Bank Note Printing Office.

But is the stamp an error of color or a proof? The normal 5o was printed in yellow-green, although varieties also are known in blue-green. The rarity is printed in brown, the same color as the 3o, which leads many collectors to believe a sheet of the 5o was printed in the wrong color.

However, Nils Farnstrom, writing in the British *Philatelic Magazine* in January 1984, says the 5o brown is a color proof that was sent by mistake to some foreign postal administrations.

Farnstrom explains that when the 3Oo brown was being printed, the ink was used to make a proof of the 5o. He says this proof sheet was mixed in with the 3Oo sheets and broken up. The Swedish Post Office sent 55 copies of the 5o proofs to foreign postal administrations. The Swedish Philatelic Society (Sveriges Philatelist Forbund) agrees with Farnstrom. The society takes the position that the 5o brown was made on "proof" paper, which was the same watermarked paper used for the issued stamps.

The society maintains that 55 copies were sent to foreign postal administrations. Over the years, the postal administrations gave copies of these proofs to various individuals.

In 1905, seven copies remained in the Swedish Post Office inventory. These have since been dispersed.

One used copy exists. It is postmarked January 1, 1894. The Scott catalog lists mint copies at $7,000. Christie's sold a copy of this rarity at its May 13, 1987, auction. Described as an "error of color," it realized 3,600 Swiss francs (about $2,500).

Several used copies exist that have been chemically changed to resemble the 5o brown.

Off to the Races

VALUE: $5,500

The Swiss 10-centime+15c inverted surcharge error has been traced to a car rally in Baden, Germany.

One of Switzerland's greatest modern rarities occurred on a surcharged airmail issue of 1935-38. In the 1930s, several European countries agreed to uniform rates for airmail postage. The new Swiss airmail rates were 20 centimes for postcards to destinations within the confederation, 30c for postcards to foreign destinations, and 40c for letters to European destinations.

Stamps in multiples of 10c would make up these rates. The Swiss Posts, Telephones and Telegraphs surcharged six airmail stamps with new values to meet these rates. Among these surcharged issues was the 10c-on-15c Disarmament Conference issue, which would prove to be its most versatile stamp. This stamp also brought philatelic attention to a car rally, an event that otherwise would have been lost in history, at least to stamp collectors.

On August 15, 1937, the Swiss Post Office sent its mobile post office van to the Baden Motor Rally to sell stamps. Under ordinary circumstances, this would have been considered a non-event by collectors. But, as it turned out, the clerk at this mobile post office was selling what was to become one of the great Swiss rarities.

Swiss postal regulations permitted airmail stamps to be used for

129

ordinary mail, so the surcharged airmail issues were being sold by the mobile post office van. A customer purchased one of the 10c-on-15c and noticed it featured an upside down surcharge. When collectors learned of the discovery, they rushed to the counter, anxious to purchase a copy of the error. Supplies were quickly exhausted.

It is not known how many copies of the error were sold that day, but it is believed only one sheet of 50 ever existed. These inverted surcharge errors have been traced to the mobile post office at the Baden Motor Rally because of two postcards bearing stamps with the inverted surcharges. These are the only two cards known to exist. Fred R. Lesser described these in the February 1980 issue of the *American Philatelist*. Lesser says both cards bear the blue "PAR AVION" label, indicating that the senders designated the cards to be sent by airmail. He says one was addressed to Baden, although Baden had no airport. The other was mailed to Bottstein, a small village in the Canton of Argau.

Despite the airmail markings, neither card was flown. They were carried by the mobile post office van to Zurich, where they received the "Zurich-Luftpost" cancel.

One card, which probably was given away as publicity by Saurer AG, the manufacturer of the postal van, bears two copies of the inverted surcharge error. The other, a card commemorating the reconstruction of an ancient castle, is franked with a block of four of the error. The stamps on both cards are canceled with the "1 SCHWEIZ AUTOMOBIL-POSTBUREAU *" postmark dated August 15, 1937. A small number of mint errors also exist.

Lesser describes how the errors were created. He says that to ensure good registration of the surcharge, the top and right margins were removed from each sheet of stamps, and the perforated edges were employed for batch alignment. However, a single sheet was placed in the stack upside down and received the surcharges inverted in relation to the stamp design. He says proof of this are the mint inverted surcharge copies with the top and/or right margin still intact.

An example with the right margin was sold in the Harmers of London auction of the "Pegasus" airmail collection March 11-12, 1986, for £3,410 (about $5,000). Scott catalog lists the 10c-on-15c inverted surcharge error at $5,500 mint and $8,500 used.

Laid-Paper Varieties

VALUE: $3,190

The Tasmania 1853 4-penny "Van Diemen's Land" stamp on laid paper.

The Dutch explorer Abel Janszoon Tasman discovered the island of Tasmania in 1642 and named it Van Diemen's Land in honor of Anthony van Diemen, governor-general of the Dutch East India Company. No attempt was made to establish a settlement on the island until 1803 when it was used as a penal colony.

In the late 1840s, settlers began inhabiting Van Diemen's Land, and by 1853, a need for postage stamps became apparent. The Post Office Act of 1853 ordered the prepayment of all letters and packages by adhesive stamps.

The colony issued two imperforate stamps November 1, 1853. C.W. Coard engraved both in plates of 24 stamps (four horizontal rows of six). They feature a profile of Queen Victoria facing right.

The 1 penny shows the portrait in an oval within a rectangular frame. The corners of the stamp are cut out. The format of the 4d is octagonal.

H. and C. Best printed the stamps on a press at the offices of the local newspaper, *Courier*. Since Coard engraved each stamp by hand, each features minor varieties, making it possible to plate this issue. This makes these early stamps popular with collectors.

A major variety of the 4d exists. The normal 1d and 4d stamps were printed on wove paper which varies from a medium soft paper to a thin, hard paper. However, the 4d also exists on laid paper.

When this variety first appeared, collectors believed it to be a proof because no used copies exist. It still is not certain why copies of this stamp were printed on laid paper. This scarce variety catalogs in Scott at $10,000. Christie's/Robson Lowe sold a copy for $3,190, including a 10-percent buyer's premium, at its March 11, 1987, Isleham sale.

In *Stamps of Great Price*, Nevile Stocken recalls selling a sheet of 24 of the 4d on laid paper. It was consigned by Coard's daughter. Stocken said it realized a disappointing £800 at the time.

He said the family also owned a sheet of the 1d blue. They had framed both sheets and hung them on the wall in their home in Tasmania. When they later moved to India, the sheet of 1d was stolen off the walls of their bungalow, according to Stocken.

The 1d and normal 4d also are expensive. The total printings were 250,000 1d and 800,000 4d. Scott lists the 1d at $5,500 mint and $1,000 used, and the 4d at $3,500 mint and $650 used.

Two plates were used for the printing of the 4d. The first state of plate I shows finely engraved lines. The second state shows signs of wear. Plate II features coarse engraving with much thicker lines.

Reprints of both values were made from plates defaced with two thick strokes across the queen's head. Some show the word "REPRINT." Some reprints are perforated 11½; others are imperforate like the normal stamps.

In 1855, these locally produced issues were replaced with beautifully printed stamps produced by Perkins Bacon in London featuring the Chalon head of Queen Victoria.

TOBAGO

A Curlicue '1'

VALUE: $16,500
A copy of Tobago's 6-penny bisect with the 1d manuscript surcharge.

    The islands of the British West Indies created numerous bisects in the 19th century. One of the scarcest of these bisects comes from Tobago, an island lying off the Venezuelan coast.
    The British administered Tobago as a separate colony until 1896 when the island was united with nearby Trinidad to form the colony of Trinidad and Tobago.
    Tobago issued its first stamps in 1879. On August 1 of that year, a set of revenue stamps, already in use for fiscal purposes, was introduced for postage. Thomas De La Rue in England engraved the stamps, which feature a diademed portrait of Queen Victoria. As was typical with many of the early British colonial issues, one keyplate was used for the central design for all values. De La Rue used separate duty plates to print the values.

The stamps bear the country name and the value. Since they originally were intended for revenue purposes only, the stamps carry no reference to postage.

These stamps continued in use until December 31, 1880. However, a shortage of the 1-penny value arose.

To fill this need for 1d stamps, Tobago followed the lead of many other islands in the British West Indies. It surcharged and bisected an issue. The 6-penny stamp was cut in half and surcharged with a manuscript 1d. To collectors unfamiliar with British markings, this surcharge may appear strange. It looks like an "i" dotted with a curlicue. Actually, it is a "1" with the "d," the abbreviation for penny, printed above it.

Mint copies of this 1d-on-6d provisional bisect are extremely scarce. Even the Royal Collection, which contains examples of most British colonial rarities, is missing a mint copy of this provisional. The stamp usually commands a five-figure price when sold today. The Scott catalog lists it at $12,500 mint and $2,000 used.

In 1983, Colonial Stamp Company sold a mint copy of the provisional at its November 14 auction for $10,000. This example is the right half of the 6d stamp. It was once in the Arthur Hind collection. It was sold in 1934 and later was part of the Mathis and Cox collections. The manuscript provisional on a left half was sold by Colonial at its September 30, 1987, auction. It realized $16,500, including the 10-percent buyer's premium. The Colonial auction catalog for this auction refers to sales in which two copies of this provisional realized $19,800 each.

On December 31, Tobago issued a new set of stamps. Once again, they featured a diademed portrait of Queen Victoria. But this time the inscription read "TOBAGO/POSTAGE."

TRANSVAAL

Printing Shenanigans

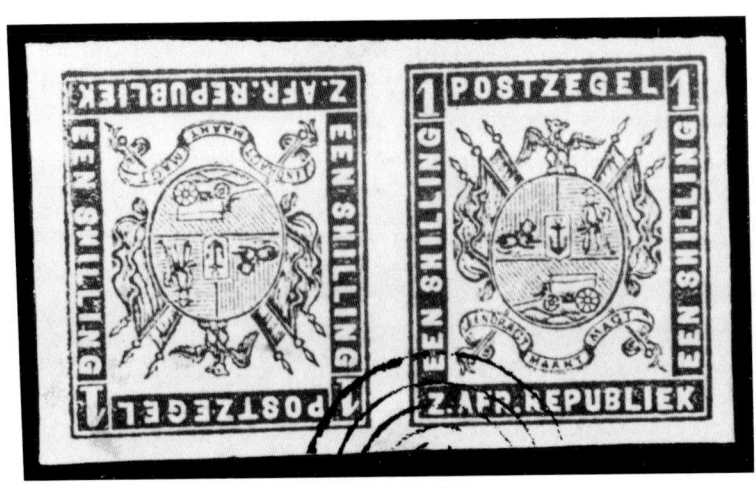

VALUE: $6,500

An example of a 1/- tete-beche pair of the Boer republic of Transvaal.

A devious German printer was behind the creation of the tete-beche rarities of the Boer republic of Transvaal (now the Republic of South Africa).

Transvaal issued its first postage stamps in 1869. Postmaster General Fred Jeppe, a German, ordered the country's first stamps from Adolph Otto, a printer in Mecklenburg Schwerin, Germany.

Even in the 1860s, postmasters realized the financial potential of postage stamps. Transvaal's treasury needed to be fattened, and Jeppe found a way to fatten it — through stamp collectors.

Transvaal's first stamps — known as the Mecklenburgs — were issued with stamp collectors in mind. Jeppe was quoted several years later as saying that none of the Mecklenburgs was on sale to the public. They were all sold to collectors. In fact, most were sold to collectors. Some never made it to Transvaal. Otto sold them directly to stamp dealers to try to recoup debts owed to him by the Transvaal government.

But Otto's shenanigans did not stop with selling stamps to dealers. He also created counterfeit trial impressions and reprints.

In producing the plates for Transvaal's first issue, Otto inverted the stamp subjects on some positions of the 6-penny and 1/- plates. Whether this was deliberate or accidental may never be known, but it resulted in tete-beche pairs. In tete-beche pairs, one stamp is in the normal upright position; the other is upside down. The tete-beche pairs of Transvaal are extremely rare, particularly the 1/- of 1869.

Although Transvaal canceled its contract with Otto and began using African printers, the same plates produced by Otto were used for later issues printed in Africa. Therefore, the tete-beche pairs occur not only in the Mecklenburg printing but also in the various issues of the first republic and the first British occupation.

The Scott catalog lists the Transvaal 1869 1/- tete-beche pair at $15,000 mint. Tete-beche pairs of the later printings catalog from $4,500 to $12,500.

A 1/- tete-beche pair from the first British occupation is in the Royal Collection in Buckingham Palace.

Collectors are cautioned that Otto created many forgeries of Transvaal issues, including tete-beche pairs. Genuine copies seldom come on the market. Transvaal forgeries are covered extensively in *Transvaal Philately* by Major Ian B. Mathews.

Asia Minor Gems

VALUE: $4,500 **VALUE: $2,100**

The Asia Minor Steamship Company stamps were issued about 1868.

The stamps and postal history associated with the steamships that have plied the waters of the world fascinate collectors. Steamship companies have issued stamps and special postmarks. Some of these stamps and postmarks, as well as the covers bearing them, are extremely scarce.

Among these rarities are the Asia Minor Steamship Company stamps. Little is known about these stamps, but this only adds to their attractiveness and to their value.

The Asia Minor Steamship Company was founded in 1868 in the Turkish port of Smyrna (now Izmir). The company's ships sailed between Smyrna and Adalia, calling at various ports along the way.

What little information that is known about the Asia Minor Steamship Company and its stamps is detailed in *The Private Ship Letter Stamps of the World — Part 2: Australia-Europe-South America* by S. Ringstrom and H.E. Tester. The authors said the company owned two steamers — *Bellona* and *Tzoura*. The *Tzoura* was wrecked in the English Channel after being repaired in Britain.

The Asia Minor Steamship Company, whose ships operated under the British flag, issued two stamps. Fewer than 30 examples of these stamps exist today. The company issued two denominations — 1 piastre and 2pi. The 2pi seems to have covered the normal letter rate. The 1pi is the scarcer of the two.

Both rectangular stamps are believed to have been printed in England. They are lithographed in black on white paper with an emerald green glazed surface. They each carry the inscription "ASIA MINOR/S.S.Co." as the central design with the denomination below — either "ONE PIASTRE" or "2 PIASTRES." This inscription is bordered by an ornamental frame.

The Asia Minor Steamship Company stamps were first mentioned in *Le Timbre Poste* in February 1879. Little is known about these stamps. Collectors have been unable to determine when they were first issued and when they were withdrawn from use. In *Rare Stamps*, noted writers L.N. and M. Williams said the stamps were issued in about 1868 and were in use for only a year or two.

What is known is that these stamps are extremely scarce, particularly used on cover. The 2pi is known used on cover.

The Williams brothers mentioned a vertical pair of the 1pi exists.

Two examples of the steamship company stamps are in the Tapling collection at the British Museum.

In its October 16-22, 1983 auction, David Feldman SA sold two examples of the Asia Minor rarities. A 1pi realized 9,775 Swiss francs (approximately $4,500). A 2pi realized 4,600fr ($2,100).

An Assortment of Settings

VALUE: $7,150
The ½d-on-1/- slate blue, setting c, of the Turks Islands provisionals.

The Turks Islands boasts several gems among its early issues. The islands are a British possession in the West Indies, lying southeast of the Bahamas and north of Haiti.

Postage stamps inscribed "Turks and Caicos Islands" have been used since 1900, Caicos being a group of islands northwest of the Turks. Prior to 1900 and in recent years, separate stamps were issued for the Turks Islands.

In the early days, the captains of vessels that came to call on the islands were entrusted with the mail. In 1867, the Turks Islands issued its first postage stamps. The design featured a portrait of Queen Victoria facing left. The stamps were engraved by Perkins, Bacon in England and printed on unwatermarked paper.

In 1873, the islands introduced a new set of stamps on paper watermarked with a star. It is to this second set that one of the Turks Islands' rarest stamps belongs. Only a small quantity of the 1/- violet was produced. Few exist today in mint condition. The

Scott catalog lists this stamp at $10,000 mint and $3,750 used.

The islands joined the Universal Postal Union in 1881, making new denominations necessary. Since the printer in England could not produce new stamps in time, the islands resorted to commissioning a local printer to surcharge the stamps that were in use at the time. The printer created a plethora of surcharge varieties using various typefaces and settings. Twelve settings of the ½ penny, nine of the 2½d and six of the 4d exist.

Many of the 1/- violet were surcharged, thus adding to the scarcity of the unsurcharged issue. Extremely rare is the 2½d-on-1/- provisional with what the Scott catalog refers to as the type j surcharge. It catalogs at $10,000 mint.

Another scarce issue is the ½d-on-1/- slate blue. It catalogs at $15,000. An example of this stamp sold at Christie's sale of the Isleham collection March 11, 1987, for $7,150, including the 10-percent buyer's premium.

Other rarities include the 2½d-on-6d and 2½d-on-1/- provisionals, both with surcharge setting k. They catalog at $11,000 mint. The 2½-on-1/- slate blue with setting n is listed in the Scott catalog at $10,000. Scarce varieties include the horizontal pair imperforate between of the 2½d-on-6d gray black with setting g, the same stamp with a double surcharge, and the 2½d-on-1/- with setting m with the fraction bar omitted.

UNITED STATES

A Unique Carrier

VALUE: $11,000 plus

This cover to Brunswick, Georgia, bears the only recorded copy of the Beckman's City Post carrier stamp. The 2¢ stamp was issued in 1860.

Only one copy of the Beckman's City Post carrier stamp has been recorded. This is only one of several carrier stamps issued for Charleston, South Carolina. Carrier stamps prepaid the fees of officially bonded letter carriers who were appointed by the postmaster general of the United States.

Threatened by private mail-carrying systems in the 1840s and 1850s, the U.S. Post Office Department convinced Congress to declare all city streets as U.S. post roads in 1851. Postmasters hired officially bonded letter carriers to carry mail to and from the post offices within the area for which the stamps were issued.

Two official carrier stamps were released by the U.S. Post Office Department. Several semiofficial carrier stamps were issued either directly by or sanctioned by the local postmasters. The Beckman's City Post issue falls under the semiofficial category.

Unlike the carrier stamps of most cities, those of Charleston, South Carolina, are well-documented, thanks to W.H. Faber, who was a resident of the city at the time the carrier services operated. The Charleston carrier services spanned a period from 1849, prior to the Congressional decision regarding post roads, to about 1865.

In 1849, Postmaster General Jacob Collamer appointed John H. Honour as Charleston's letter carrier. Honour employed his brother-in-law, E.J. Kingman, as his assistant. In 1851, they separated, forming two carrier businesses. They divided the city in two — one operating the service in the eastern half of the city, the other in the western half of the city.

When Kingman retired in 1858, Joseph G. Martin replaced him. John F. Steinmeyer Jr. formed Steinmeyer's City Post the same year. Honour retired in 1860, and the postmaster general appointed John C. Beckman as Honour's replacement.

Semiofficial stamps were issued for each of these carrier services. They represented the prepayment of the carrier fees. The carrier charge in Charleston was 2¢.

The scarcest of these Charleston carrier stamps is the 2¢ issued by John C. Beckman in 1860.

The design simply features the wording "Beckman's/City Post/Paid—2cts" with an ornamental border. It is similar to the other Charleston issues.

The only copy known is on a cover franked with a U.S. 1857 3¢ red. The cover is addressed to Robert Hazlehurst in Brunswick, Georgia. The Beckman's carrier is lightly canceled by pencil. Both the carrier stamp and the 3¢ red are tied together by a "CHARLESTON S.C." postmark dated June 18, 1860.

The cover was owned by Count Ferrari, one of the world's most famous collectors. Alfred Caspary bought this rarity to add to his worldwide collection. When Caspary's collection of U.S. carriers and locals was sold in 1957, the cover sold for $11,000.

UNITED STATES

The Omaha Error

VALUE: $25,000

The block of four of the United States 8¢ Trans-Mississippi horizontally imperforate error with the bottom imprint and plate number 609.

A clerk at the main post office in Philadelphia discovered what was to become one of the United States' most widely sought errors — the 1898 8¢ part-perforated error of the Trans-Mississippi set.

The U.S. Post Office Department released the Trans-Mississippi issue, dubbed the Omaha issue by stamp collectors, to commemorate the Trans-Mississippi and International Exposition, which took place June 1 to November 1, 1898, in Omaha, Nebraska.

Although this set of stamps brought cries of protest from collectors at the time it was issued, it has become a favorite of collectors today. Contemporary collectors objected to the length of the set — nine stamps in all — and to the high-value $1 and $2 stamps. This set also followed closely on the heels of the long Columbian set.

143

James A. Gary, who was postmaster general at the time, defended the set by stating that he authorized it to "help the people of the West." He added, "No one is compelled to buy the high values unless he wishes to do so."

The Trans-Mississippi issue originally was planned as a bicolor set of stamps with the frames in various colors for each denomination and the vignettes in black. However, the Bureau of Engraving and Printing was working to full capacity to print revenue stamps to support the Spanish-American War. The U.S. Post Office abandoned the idea for bicolor stamps in favor of single-color issues that could be produced more easily.

The stamps in the Trans-Mississippi set differ from the definitives of the time in that the engraved space is about 7/8 inch wide by about 1 3/8 inches long. The ornamental borders are basically the same throughout the set, except for the values. The stamps were printed in sheets of 100 and issued in panes of 50.

The designs show western scenes, including "Marquette on the Mississippi," from a painting by Lamprecht, 1¢; "Farming in the West," from a photograph, 2¢; "Indian Hunting Buffalo," a reproduction of an engraving, 4¢; "Fremont on Rocky Mountains," from a wood engraving, 5¢; "Troops Guarding Train," from a drawing by Frederic Remington, 8¢; "Hardships of Emigration," from a painting by A.G. Heaton, 10¢; "Western Mining Prospector," from another drawing by Remington, 50¢; "Western Cattle in Storm," an engraving from a picture by J. MacWhirter, $1; and "Mississippi River Bridge," from an engraving, $2.

Robert Watts, a clerk at the main post office in Philadelphia, opened a bundle of the Trans-Mississippi stamps for distribution at his counter. Tucked in between the wrapping paper he discovered a pane of 50 with the horizontal perforations missing.

These horizontally formatted stamps had to pass twice through the perforating machine. This part-perf pane passed through the machine only once.

George B. Sloane told the story of the pane's discovery in *The Stamp Specialist*. Lester Brookman expanded on the story in his *The United States Postage Stamps of the 19th Century*.

Watt discovered the pane, which was the right pane of plate 609. He sold it to Herman Lewin, a local locksmith, for double the face value. Lewin sold it to William S.F. Pierce, also of Philadelphia. That was the last time the pane was sold intact.

Pierce broke up the pane and divided it into a vertical strip of 10 with the sheet margin and full arrow marking at right, a vertical block of 20 showing the Bureau imprint and plate number at both top and bottom, and a vertical block of 20 with the straightedge down the left side showing a half-arrow marking at top and bottom.

Pierce resold the vertical strip of 10 to Lewin for $15. Lewin took the strip home to Holland with him. It later was sold in Europe,

VALUE: $12,000
A vertical pair of the 8¢ Omaha part-perf error with a right sheet margin.

where it remained for several years.

The strip returned to the United States and was broken up. Ethel B. McCoy, who also owned a block of the 24¢ inverted Jenny, bought the right-arrow strip of four from the strip for $4,000.

Sloane said the vertical block of 20 stamps with the straightedge at left was sold to a Philadelphia dealer, Arthur Tuttle. Tuttle broke up the block, selling pairs of the error for $10 each. John N. Luff bought one such pair. A block of four from the Tuttle block, showing one of the half arrows, was in the Miller collection at the New York Public Library. Fortunately, it was not among the stamps stolen from the library in the 1970s.

Pierce kept the other block of 20 stamps for a time. He then sold the top and bottom plate number blocks of four to Albert W. Batchelder of the New England Stamp Company in Boston for $175. Pierce gave a block of four to a friend, William E. Dobbins of Philadelphia. When Dobbins died, his collection was sold to Edgar L. Green, also of Philadelphia. Pierce later disposed of his remaining two blocks of four, probably to Batchelder.

The block of four with the bottom imprint and plate number 609 was in the Colonel E.H.R. Green collection when it was sold by Harmer, Rooke & Company March 25-29, 1946.

This block was sold at the October 27, 1983, "Quality" auction by Harmers of New York. It realized $25,000, including the 10-percent buyer's premium.

The same year, Robert A. Siegel Auction Galleries sold a right sheet margin vertical pair of the part-perf error for $15,500, including the 10-percent buyer's premium.

In a more recent sale, Daniel Kelleher, Inc., sold a pair at its September 9-10, 1987, auction for $11,000, including the buyer's premium. The Scott catalog lists the pairs at $12,000.

UNITED STATES

Endwise and Sidewise

VALUE: $35,000
The scarcest of the U.S. coils — the 2¢ carmine Washington endwise coil.

VALUE: $22,500
A 1¢ blue-green endwise coil was created from regular sheet stamps.

The scarcity of the first coil stamps of the United States can be attributed to collectors' fear of fakes. In 1908, the U.S. Post Office Department issued its first coils as an experiment. They were produced from regular sheets of 400 stamps.

147

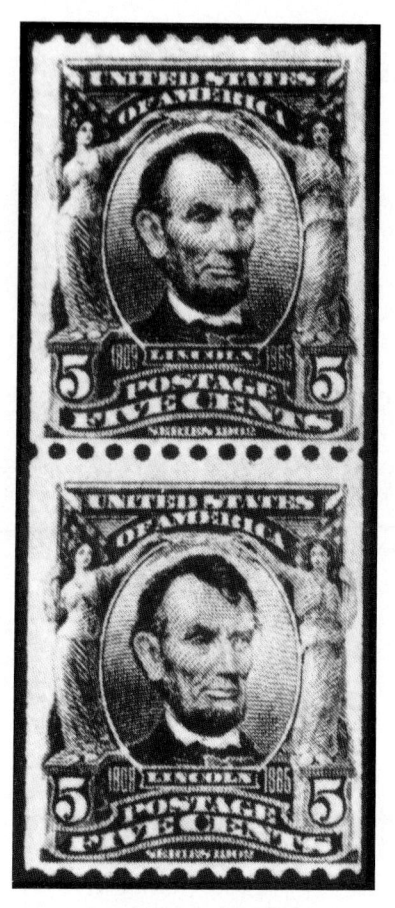

VALUE: $5,500
A copy of the more common U.S. 5¢ blue Lincoln endwise coil stamp.

    The stamps were perforated 12 in the horizontal gutters between the stamps and then cut vertically into strips of 20. These strips then were pasted together endwise (one stamp above the other) to create rolls of 500 and 1,000.
    The Post Office Department released 1¢ green and 2¢ carmine coils on February 18, 1908. The 1¢ portrays Benjamin Franklin; the 2¢, George Washington. The 2¢ is extremely scarce. Scott catalog lists it at $35,000 mint for a pair. The 1¢ catalogs at $22,500. Daniel

Kelleher auctioned a 1¢ endwise coil at its September 30-October 1, 1986, sale. The coil realized $16,500, including a 10-percent buyer's premium.

The scarcity of these coils can be directly linked to the ease with which they could be faked. Since they were created from sheet stamps, regular issues — especially booklet stamps which already

VALUE: $5,500
An example of the 1908 2¢ carmine George Washington sidewise coil.

VALUE: $4,250
A sidewise coil of the United States, the 1908 1¢ blue-green Ben Franklin.

had one side imperforate — could be trimmed to resemble the coils. One means of detecting these fakes is the watermark. The letters of the watermark on genuine coils read horizontally. The watermark is vertical on those produced from booklet stamps. Collectors feared adding faked coils to their collection, so they ignored the stamps. Few were preserved, contributing to their rarity today.

Another endwise coil was issued February 24, 1908. This 5¢ blue stamp, portraying Abraham Lincoln, was issued to cover the foreign rate. Scott lists pairs of this value at $5,500 mint.

On July 31, the Post Office Department issued its first sidewise coils. These stamps were perforated 12 vertically. The 1¢ blue-green features Franklin. The 2¢ carmine shows Washington.

Since most of the vending machines used stamps perforated vertically, these saw wider use than the endwise coils. Collectors took more interest in these sidewise coils because they were not as easy to fake. While expensive, these stamps are more common than their endwise counterparts. The 1¢ is listed in Scott at $5,500; the 2¢ at $4,250. Guideline pairs of all these coils command much higher prices. A guideline pair of the 1¢ endwise coil realized $12,375, including a 10-percent buyer's premium, at Steve Ivy's AMERIPEX auction on May 26, 1986.

Collectors did not actively pursue coils until the Post Office issued them perf 8½ in 1910. No other stamps existed in that perf measurement, so collectors felt safer adding these coils to their albums. The fear of fakes was alleviated.

UNITED STATES

An Unwatermarked Rarity

VALUE: Indeterminable

This mint plate number block of six of the U.S. 30¢ orange-red perforated 10 is from the original discovery pane found in Jim Hughes' collection.

One of the most controversial United States rarities is the 1916-17 30¢ orange-red perforated 10 on unwatermarked paper. The stamp is listed in the Scott catalog as 476A. Much of the debate stems from the fact that it is difficult to determine if a single copy of this stamp is watermarked or not.

In his *The United States Postage Stamps of the 20th Century*, Max G. Johl, a well-known collector of U.S. stamps, denied the existence of the unwatermarked version of the 30¢ perf 10. Johl said that the Bureau of Engraving and Printing, the printers of the 30¢ Franklin stamps, confirmed that this denomination perforated

10 on unwatermarked paper "could not exist as the 30¢ plates did not go to press between the time the Bureau started using unwatermarked paper and the time that the last flat plate perforating machine had been changed to 11 gauge."

Johl further stated that a "checkup on the 'unwatermarked' stamps with the aid of photography showed the watermark to be present but very faint."

Many collectors took Johl's word as gospel until in the late 1930s a new discovery was made. Herman Herst Jr. has frequently told the story of the discovery of the first sheet of Scott 476A.

Jim Hughes was an old-time collector and accumulator who lived in Linwood, New Jersey. Hughes died in the late 1930s. When his collection was being prepared for dispersal, sheets of early 20th-century U.S. stamps were found.

Upon closer examination, it was discovered that Hughes owned a full pane of 100 of the unwatermarked 30¢ perf 10. No trace of watermark could be found on the stamps or on the margins, where the watermark could be expected to be most visible.

A Boston dealer bought the pane. The pane lent credence to the existence of Scott 476A.

That is, until the early 1980s. In its 1983 U.S. Specialized, the Scott Publishing Company added a disclaimer under 476A stating that the stamp was not regularly issued and was of questionable status. Scott heard outcries from many collectors, particularly those who owned copies of 476A. Stamp dealer Jack Molesworth wrote in *Linn's Stamp News* that "while the comment was placed in the 1983 edition of the Scott Specialized catalog at the formal request of the chairman of the Philatelic Foundation Expert Committee, the overall membership of the committee was apparently not consulted before that request was communicated to Scott Publishing Company." Molesworth said, "That request by the PF is quite perplexing in light of the PF having certified as genuine two full panes of 100 of Scott 476A and other pieces and blocks, as well as singles from the panes."

Scott deleted the notation in its 1984 catalog. Today, the Scott catalog lists the stamp but gives no prices.

Robert A. Siegel's 1988 Rarities of the World sale, which took place April 23, featured a single and two blocks. The single realized $1,430. A mint block from the Hughes discovery pane sold for $17,050. Both prices include a 10-percent buyer's premium.

UNITED STATES

Blame The Clerk

VALUE: $2,250 plus
This block of four of the imperforate 2¢ Von Steuben was part of the Lilly collection when it was sold by Siegel Auction Galleries in 1967.

    An honest post office clerk reduced the number of a United States imperforate variety available to collectors by returning the imperf stamps to the post office.
    The U.S. Post Office issued a 2¢ stamp on September 17, 1930, to honor General Frederick Wilhelm Von Steuben. The Bureau of

Engraving and Printing produced the stamps from flat plates of 400 subjects. These were divided into post office panes of 100 and perforated 11. One sheet of 400, however, was only partially perforated. Two panes from this sheet were completely imperforate.

In December 1930, a postal clerk discovered a part-perforated pane of the Von Steuben stamp in his stock. The clerk contacted the Reverend L.A. Boone, a local stamp collector, and offered to sell the pane to him. Boone jumped at the opportunity, but a few days later, he received a telegram from the clerk asking him to return the pane. It seems the clerk's conscience bothered him. He explained to Boone that he had found that it was against postal regulations for a postal employee to profit from selling stamps. Boone returned the pane to the post office.

The clerk then contacted the U.S. Post Office Department, requesting permission to keep the pane. He was told to return it to Washington for destruction. He obeyed the order.

In describing this pane in 1931, Boone said, "The collectors of stamps lost one of the prettiest error items it has been my good fortune to see in over 20 years of active collecting. Only 15 stamps were cut by the perforation, and they were fairly well pasted back in position with gum tape. The remainder of the sheet was perfect, no breaks, tears or pencil marks."

A second pane also was discovered at the Midland Post Office. This pane was entirely imperforate. A hotel bought the pane from the post office in the normal course of business.

Hotel employees diligently cut the stamps apart each time one was sold. However, they soon grew tired of this, and the hotel returned the balance of the pane to the post office. Seventy stamps from this pane were used on the mail. The remainder of the pane was returned to Washington and destroyed.

A third pane was found in a post office in the state of Washington. This was later broken up into pairs and blocks of four and six.

Collectors believe the fourth pane from the sheet was destroyed by Bureau inspectors.

Only 50 imperf pairs are believed to exist today. The Scott catalog lists them at $2,250. A plate number margin block of six catalogs $10,000. A block of four of the imperf 2¢ Von Steuben was part of the Josiah K. Lilly collection when it was sold by Robert A. Siegel Auction Galleries in 1967.

The Stagecoach Stamps

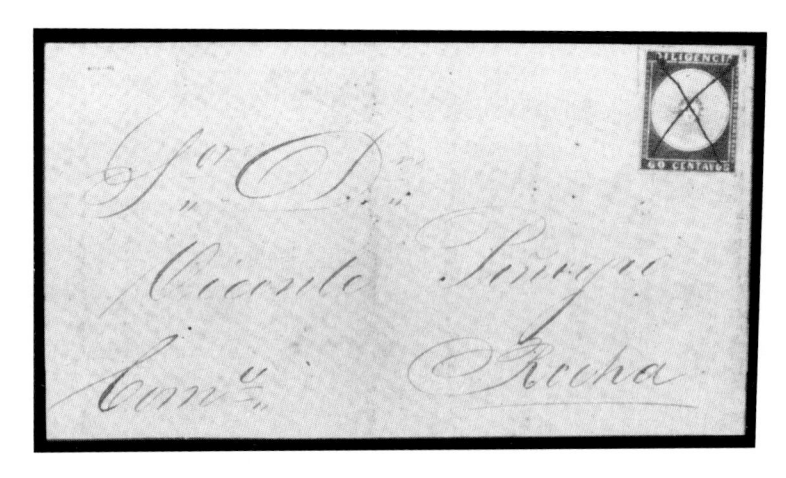

VALUE: Indeterminable

This cover, one of the most famous bearing the Uruguay 1857 60-centavo Diligencia issue, was found in the Vincente Pineyro correspondence.

Uruguay's Diligencia issues are among that country's most sought-after stamps. But one of these is an outstanding rarity.

In the early 1850s, Atanasio Lapido carried Uruguayan mail on his stagecoach lines. In 1856, Lapido was appointed postmaster general of Uruguay. He took advantage of his position and issued a set of three stamps to frank mail carried on his stagecoaches.

The central design of the stamps features a rayed sun with a human face, taken from the Uruguay coat of arms. "DILIGENCIA" (Spanish for stagecoach) appears at the top; the value — 60 centavos, 80c or 1 real — is at the bottom. The stamps were lithographed in sheets of 35 by Senors Mege y Willems. The two higher values were produced by altering the value on the 60c stone.

Because the 60c was the most popular rate, supplies of this stamp were quickly exhausted. In 1857, Lapido ordered a new supply of this denomination. This second type is the great rarity of this issue.

Fausto Diaz Paulos described the distinguishing characteristics of the two types of the 60c in an article in the June 1979 *American Philatelist*. The first type features 105 rays, a wide face, short hair,

VALUE: $2,750
Unused example of the second type of the rare Uruguay 60c Diligencia.

and a Greek guard border at each side. The second type has 67 rays, a thin face, long hair, and borders consisting of 20 pairs of vertical dashes. The width of "DILIGENCIA" is 11.7 millimeters in type I and 14.7mm in type II. The letters on type II are spaced wider apart than on type I.

Genuinely used copies of either type are scarce, but the 1857 type II stamps are especially rare used. About 10 covers exist. Mint copies are listed in Scott catalog at $2,500.

The normal color for the 60c is blue, but two varieties — pale blue and dark blue — exist. Scott lists these at $2,750. The catalog lists no price for used copies because so few have come on the market. Most used copies are pen canceled.

One of the most famous of the 1857 60c Diligencia covers was discovered by Anselmo Seijo in the correspondence of Vicente Pineyro of Rocha, Uruguay. This cover was purchased by Vincent Ferrer and was illustrated in Hugo Griebert's *A Study of the Stamps of Uruguay*, published in 1910.

The cover later was purchased by Remigio Sciarra, a noted collector of Uruguay. It then was bought by Alfred Lichtenstein and was part of the collection bequeathed to his daughter, Louise Boyd Dale. The cover was sold during the Dale-Lichtenstein auctions in 1969 by H.R. Harmer.

The only known multiple of this issue is a pair on a cover addressed to General Diego Lamas. It was sent to Lamas by General Leandro Gomez in 1859.

Forgeries of the second type 60c exist. In his article, Paulos calls special attention to those produced by the famed forger Jean de Sperati. He says Sperati borrowed a copy of the genuine stamp from Robert Hoffman to use as a model. He says the Sperati forgeries have a broken left eyebrow and a thick upper margin.

URUGUAY

An Upside-Down Amazon

VALUE: $1,100
Only used copies exist of this 1895 25-centesimo inverted-center error.

Most inverted-center errors exist only in mint condition. The error is usually so striking that it is easily recognized. Even non-collectors would hesitate to use such a stamp to mail a letter.

An exception, however, is a South American rarity from Uruguay. This inverted-center error exists only in used condition. Apparently, no one recognized the value of this stamp before licking it and sticking it on an envelope.

But this may have added to the stamp's rarity. Many ended up in the wastebasket; few copies have survived.

The 25-centesimo stamp of Uruguay's 1895-99 series features a portrait of an Amazon. (Scott catalog refers to the figure as "Liberty.") Waterlow and Sons in England engraved this series of definitives. The 25c was printed in two colors — red-brown and black.

During the second pass through the press, a sheet of the 25c was turned upside down, resulting in inverted centers. Inspectors at the printer failed to catch the error. It was not until about 40 copies had been sold at the post office that the inverted centers were discovered. Once alerted to the existence of the errors, the Uruguayan Post Office immediately withdrew this issue from sale. Remaining copies of the error were destroyed.

Most of those sold were used for postage by people who were unaware that they had purchased a rarity during their visit to the post office. The number of these errors was further diminished by those that were thrown into the wastebasket by unsuspecting recipients. No mint copies exist. The Scott catalog lists the 25c inverted-center error at $2,250.

An example of this error sold for $1,100, including a 10-percent buyer's premium, at the March 12, 1987, auction conducted by Christie's. The stamp was part of the Isleham collection.

A School Tax

VALUE: Indeterminable
Venezuela's scarce 2-centavo inverted frame variety appears in the upper right-hand stamp of this block of four. The block formerly was in the Dale-Lichtenstein collection.

In 1870, Venezuela issued an official decree authorizing stamps for prepayment of postage, as well as for revenue purposes. Two rarities exist among these stamps. Known as the First Escuelas issue of 1871-76, these stamps portray Simon Bolivar facing right. Each is overprinted "Bolivar Sucre Miranda — Decreto de 27 de Abril de 1870" or "Decreto de 27 de Junio 1870" in tiny letters across the stamp. The "Junio" overprint is continuously repeated in four lines consisting of two pairs, with the second line of each pair inverted.

As revenue stamps, this issue served to collect taxes for building and maintaining public schools. As postage stamps, the First Escuelas were the only stamps available from March 1871 until August 1873. These imperforate stamps were lithographed in Caracas by Felix Rasco, Enrique Neun, Gabriel Jose Aramburu or Remathed & Neun. Three different overprints and eight separate printings exist. Varieties are numerous, as would be expected. The three overprint types include an overprint in two double lines of upright letters; overprint in one double line of slanting script letters; and overprint in two double lines of slanting script letters. Two major errors — the 2-centavo and 15-real stamps with the frame inverted — make this issue particularly fascinating to collec-

VALUE: $2,530
A used example of the scarce 15-real inverted frame error from Venezuela, also ex-Dale-Lichtenstein.

tors. The 2c occurred during the fifth printing in 1874 by Rasco. The 15r occurred during the eighth printing in 1876, also by Rasco. This stamp is the scarcer of the two errors because the invert occurs only once in the sheet. Examples of the 15r inverted frame, therefore, are extremely hard to find.

Christie's auctioned a used copy of this error during its March 12, 1987, sale of the Latin American portion of the Isleham collection. The stamp realized $2,530, including the 10-percent buyer's premium. What makes this copy especially nice is that it is tied to a small piece by a Maracaibo company cancel dated February 23, 1878. The majority of the First Escuelas are pen-canceled because few cities in Venezuela had canceling machines at that time.

Christie's also sold an example of the 2c invert for $572 during the same sale.

Alfred Lichtenstein, one of the great American collectors, owned several copies of the First Escuelas inverts, including the 15r that was sold by Christie's.

His collection also featured an unused strip of three with the 2c invert in the center and a block of four showing the 2c inverted frame variety in the top right stamp. The strip and block were sold as part of the Dale-Lichtenstein collection by H.R. Harmers in 1969.

The Scott catalog lists the 15r invert at $8,000 mint and $6,500 used, and the 2c at $4,000 mint and $3,000 used.

Index

Volume numbers in this index refer to previous volumes in the *Philatelic Gems* series. Page numbers refer to *Philatelic Gems 4*.

Argentina 1862 15-centavo
tete-beche................. Volume 2
Argentina 1864-72 Rivadavias... Volume 1
Australia 1855 4-penny inverted
Swan..................... Volume 1
Australia 1879 4-penny missing
surcharge................. Volume 1
Australia 1897 Lake Lefroy local.. Volume 2
Australia 1915-24 2½-penny missing
numerator................. Page 1
Australia 1920 Ross Smith label.. Volume 2
Australia 1932-33 6-penny inverted
overprint.................... Page 3
Austria 1850 9-kreuzer
manuscript................ Volume 3
Austria 1852-56 Mercuries...... Volume 1
Austria 1867 3-kreuzer color
error..................... Volume 2
Baden 1851 9-kreuzer color
error..................... Volume 1
Baden 1862 Land Post......... Volume 2
Bangkok 1885 32¢-on-2-anna "B"
overprint.................... Page 7
Barbados 1863 1-shilling color
error..................... Volume 3
Barbados 1878 1-penny bisect... Volume 2
Bavaria 1849 1-kreuzer
tete-beche................. Volume 2
Bavaria 1895 Aichach
provisional................ Volume 2
Belgian Congo 1898 10-franc inverted
center.................... Page 9
Belgium 1916-18 2.50-franc
surcharge................. Volume 2
Belgium 1920 65-centime
Termonde................. Volume 2
Bermuda 1848 Perot
provisionals............... Volume 1
Bermuda 1874 3-penny-on-1d
provisional................ Page 12
Bermuda 1894 1/- imperf-between
error..................... Volume 3
Bolivia 1924 10-centavo airmail
invert.................... Page 15
Brazil 1843 Bull's-Eyes......... Volume 1
Brazil 1843 Pack strip.......... 17

Brazil 1930 5-reis Parahyba...... Volume 2
British Central Africa 1898 1-penny
invert.................... Volume 3
British Central Africa 1907 unissued
stamps.................... Volume 2
British Guiana 1850-51 2¢
Cottonreels................ Volume 1
British Guiana 1852 Patimus..... Volume 3
British Guiana 1856 1¢ magenta.. Volume 1
British Guiana 1856 4¢......... Volume 1
British Honduras 1888 2¢ black
surcharge................. Volume 2
British Solomon Islands 1939-51 2½-penny
imperforate between.......... Page 19
Buenos Aires 1859 1-peso
tete-beche................. Volume 3
Bulgaria 1879 25-centime imperf.. Page 21
Bulgaria 1882 5-stotinka color
error..................... Page 23
Bushire 1915 5-kran inverted
overprint.................... Page 25
Cameroon 1915 3/- on 3-mark
error..................... Volume 3
Canada 1851 12-penny black.... Volume 1
Canada 1851 New Carlisle
provisional................ Volume 2
Canada 1868 2¢ on laid paper... Volume 1
Canada 1899 Port Hood
provisional................ Volume 2
Canada 1927 25¢ London-to-London
semiofficial................ Volume 3
Canada 1959 5¢ Seaway invert.. Volume 1
Canal Zone 1904-25 overprints... Volume 3
Canal Zone 1947 6¢ inverted-overprint
Official................... Volume 3
Canal Zone 1962 4¢ missing
bridge.................... Volume 1
Cape of Good Hope 1853 4-penny
Triangle................... Volume 1
Cape of Good Hope 1861 1-penny, 4d
woodblock................. Volume 1
Cape of Good Hope 1900 Baden-Powell
issues.................... Page 27
Cayman Islands 1907
surcharges................ Volume 3
Ceylon 1857 6-penny plum...... Volume 3

163

Ceylon 1859 4-penny imperf . . . . . Volume 1
Chile 1854 5-centavo lithos . . . . . . Volume 2
Chile 1910 1-centavo invert. . . . . . Volume 3
China 1897 2¢-on-3-candareen doubled and inverted surcharge . . . . Page 30
China 1897 $1 small surcharge. . . Volume 2
China 1915 $2 Hall of Classics invert . . . . Volume 2
China 1941 $2 Dr. Sun Yat-sen invert . . . . Volume 3
China 1968-71 Cultural Revolution rarities . . . . Volume 2
Colombia 1859 5-centavo transfer error . . . . Volume 3
Colombia 1919 10-centavo missing surcharge . . . . Volume 3
Colombia 1919 airmail serif error . . . . Volume 2
Colombia 1920 semiofficial airmails. . . . . Volume 1
Confederate States 1861 Goliad provisionals . . . . Volume 3
Confederate States 1861 Grove Hill provisional. . . . . Volume 3
Confederate States 1861 Knoxville provisional . . . . Volume 2
Confederate States 1861 Livingston provisional. . . . . Volume 2
Confederate States 1861 Mt. Lebanon provisional. . . . . Volume 2
Confederate States 1861 Tuscumbia provisionals . . . . Volume 3
Cook Islands 1892 1-penny imperf-between. . . . . Volume 3
Cuba 1899 10¢-on-10¢ special printing. . . . . Page 32
Cyprus 1886 ½-piastre-on-½pi . . . . Page 34
Czechoslovakia 1927 50-haleru surcharge error. Volume 3
Danzig 1920 5-mark inverted overprint . . . . Volume 1
Denmark 1851 2-rigsbank-skilling . Volume 3
Dominica 1886 1-penny surcharge error. Volume 2
Egypt 1868 Suez Canal Company locals . . . . Volume 2
Falkland Islands 1964 6-penny ship error. . . . . Volume 1
Fanning Island 1911 1-penny provisional. . . . . Page 36
Faroes 1919 2-ore-on-5o invert . . . Volume 3
Fiji 1870 Fiji Times Express stamps. . . . . Volume 3
Fiji 1878-91 2-penny color error. . . Volume 3
Fiji 1922-27 2-penny missing-value error. . . . . Page 38
Finland 1850 20-kopeck stamped envelope . . . . Volume 1

Finland 1856 tete-beche pairs . . . Volume 2
Finland 1866-74 printing errors . . . Volume 3
France 1849-50 1-franc Vervelle . . . Page 40
France 1849-50 tete-beche varieties. . . . . Volume 1
France 1857 Gauthier Freres & Cie . . . . Volume 2
France 1863-70 4-centime tete-beche pair. . . . . Page 42
France 1869 5-franc missing value. Volume 2
France 1870-71 Bordeaux 20 centimes. . . . . Volume 2
France 1872-75 15-centime cliche error. . . . . Volume 3
France 1928 Catapult mail . . . . . . Volume 2
Gambia 1869 Cameo stamps . . . . Volume 1
German East Africa 1916 1-rupee Tabora. Volume 1
Germany 1900 Tientsin provisionals . . . . Volume 3
Germany 1901 3-pfennig Vineta provisional. . . . . Volume 1
Germany 1912 Gelber Hund stamps. Volume 3
Gibraltar 1889 10-centimo missing value . . . . Volume 1
Gold Coast 1883 1-penny-on-4d provisional. . . . . Volume 2
Gold Coast 1889 20/- green and red . . . . Volume 3
Great Britain 1840 House of Lords envelopes . . . . Volume 2
Great Britain 1840 Penny Black . . Volume 1
Great Britain 1840 VR Official . . . . Volume 1
Great Britain 1841 1-penny B-blank error. . . . . Volume 3
Great Britain 1864 1-penny red, plate 77 . . . . Volume 3
Great Britain 1865 9-penny plate 5 abnormal . . . . Page 44
Great Britain 1867 10-penny error of watermark . . . . Page 47
Great Britain 1867-80 6-penny plate 10 abnormal . . . . Page 49
Great Britain 1867-80 10-penny abnormal . . . . Volume 3
Great Britain 1867-82 high values . . . . Volume 2
Great Britain 1870 OP-PC errors. . Volume 2
Great Britain 1870-76 Stock Exchange forgeries . . . . Volume 2
Great Britain 1873-80 1-shilling abnormal . . . . Page 52
Great Britain 1876 Telegraph stamps. Volume 1
Great Britain 1877 4-penny vermilion abnormal . . . . Page 54

Great Britain 1880 1-penny watermark
error .... Volume 3
Great Britain 1900 "GOVT/PARCELS"
invert .... Volume 3
Great Britain 1902-04 Board of Education
Officials .... Volume 2
Great Britain 1902-04 Edward VII
Officials .... Volume 2
Great Britain 1910 2-penny Tyrian
plum .... Volume 1
Great Britain 1961 2½-penny missing
black .... Volume 2
Great Britain 1935 2½-penny prussian
blue .... Volume 2
Greece 1861 Hermes Heads ..... Volume 1
Greece 1862-67 10-lepta
salmon .... Volume 3
Greece 1871 40-lepta Solferino color
error .... Volume 1
Grenada 1875 1-penny
rough-perf 15 .... Volume 2
Grenada 1883 1-penny Gouyave
provisional .... Volume 1
Guadeloupe 1877 40-centime postage
due .... Page 56
Guatemala 1881 inverted
Quetzals .... Volume 3
Guernsey 1979 unissued
11 pence .... Page 58
Haiti 1914 50-centime overprint ... Page 60
Hawaii 1851 Missionaries .... Volume 1
Hawaii 1857 5¢-on-13¢
provisional .... Volume 3
Hawaii 1893 Provisional Government
overprints .... Page 64
Honduras 1925 Black Honduras .. Volume 1
Honduras 1925 Red Honduras ... Volume 2
India 1852 ½-anna Scinde
Dawk .... Volume 1
India 1854 4-anna inverted head .. Volume 1
India 1854 ½-anna printed on both
sides .... Page 67
Ireland 1922-23 misprinted
overprints .... Volume 2
Ireland 1935 2-penny Map coil ... Volume 2
Ireland 1976 15-penny missing color
error .... Volume 3
Isle of Man 1974 6-penny color
error .... Volume 3
Italian Offices in Ottoman Empire 1922
unissued stamp .... Page 73
Italy 1860 3-lira Tuscany
provisional .... Volume 1
Italy 1860 Garibaldi ½ tornese ... Volume 1
Italy 1865 20-centesimo-on-15c inverted
surcharge .... Page 71
Italy 1933 Balbo triptych .... Volume 1

Jamaica 1920 1/- inverted frame .. Volume 1
Jamaica 1921 unissued
6 pence .... Volume 3
Japan 1870 Sutherland locals .... Volume 1
Japan 1871 500-mon inverted
dragon .... Volume 1
Japan 1874 20 sen syllabic
character "1" .... Volume 3
Jersey 1969 10/- color error ...... Volume 3
Kenya 1954-59 5¢ inverted dam .. Volume 1
Lagos 1893 ½-penny-on-2d surcharge
error .... Page 75
Liberia 1941 airmail surcharges .. Volume 2
Lombardy-Venetia 1858 newspaper tax
stamps .... Page 5
Luxembourg 1879 "Un Pranc"
error .... Volume 3
Malta 1919 10 shillings .... Page 77
Martinique 1886-91 surcharges ... Page 79
Mauritius 1847 Post Office ...... Volume 1
Mauritius 1848-59 Post Paids .... Volume 2
Mexico 1864 Hidalgo issues ..... Volume 2
Mexico 1921 10-centavo invert ... Volume 1
Modena 1859 80-centesimo
provisional .... Volume 3
Natal 1857 first issue .... Volume 2
Natal 1857 3-penny tete-beche
pairs .... Page 81
Nauru 1916-23 10-shilling
indigo blue .... Page 83
Neapolitan Provinces 1861 color
errors .... Volume 2
Neapolitan Provinces 1861 unissued
stamps .... Volume 2
Netherlands 1894 5¢ orange color
error .... Volume 3
Netherlands 1928 9¢ missing
value .... Volume 3
Netherlands 1942 10¢-on-2½¢ missing
surcharge .... Volume 3
New Brunswick 1851 1 shilling .... Page 85
New Brunswick 1860 5¢ Connell .. Volume 1
New Hebrides 1908 1-penny missing
overprint .... Volume 3
New South Wales 1850 Sydney
Views .... Volume 2
New Zealand 1854-59 Chalon
Heads .... Volume 2
New Zealand 1906 1-penny
claret .... Page 88
New Zealand 1963 1-shilling 9-penny
missing color .... Page 90
Newfoundland 1860 1-shilling orange on laid
paper .... Page 91
Newfoundland 1919 transatlantic
overprints .... Volume 1

165

Newfoundland 1927 DePinedo
overprints .... Volume 1
Newfoundland 1930 50¢-on-36¢
Columbia .... Volume 3
Newfoundland 1932 $1.50 DO-X
invert .... Volume 3
Niger Coast 1892-94 Oil Rivers ... Volume 2
North Borneo 1922 overprint
errors .... Volume 3
Northern Nigeria 1904 £25 ...... Volume 2
Nova Scotia 1851 1/- violet ...... Volume 2
Papua 1929 3-penny airmail with overprint
omitted .... Page 94
Parma 1852 15-centesimi tete-beche
pair .... Page 69
Philippines 1944 1-peso Victory
provisional .... Page 96
Portuguese Guinea 1881 misplaced
cliche .... Page 98
Puerto Rico 1898 Ponce
provisional .... Volume 2
Reunion 1852 first issue .... Volume 2
Rhodesia 1896 Bulawayo
provisionals .... Volume 3
Rhodesia 1905 1-shilling imperforate
between .... Page 101
Romania 1858 Moldavian Bulls ... Volume 1
Russia 1857 Tiflis local .... Volume 2
Russia 1883-88 14-kopeck
bisects .... Volume 3
Russia 1902-05 7-ruble inverted
center .... Page 103
Samoa 1914 "1 shilling"
surcharge .... Volume 3
Saxony 1850 3 pfennigs .... Volume 3
Saxony 1850 3-pfennig red ...... Volume 1
Saxony 1851 ½-neugroschen paper
error .... Volume 1
Serbia 1872-79 1-para tete-beche
pair .... Page 115
Sicily 1859 ½-grana blue proof ... Volume 1
South Australia 1855 1-shilling
violet .... Page 117
South Australia 1903 "EIGNT" .. Page 119
South Georgia 1928 2½-penny
provisional .... Page 121
Spain 1851 2-real blue color error . Volume 1
Spain 1851 5-real color error ..... Volume 2
St. Helena 1868 1-shilling-on-6-penny
missing surcharge 105
St. Helena 1960 Tristan Relief .... Volume 3
St. Lucia 1869 steamship local .. Page 108
St. Vincent 1861 4-penny-on-1-shilling
provisional .... Page 113
St. Vincent 1861 6-penny
yellow-green .... Page 110
St. Vincent 1871-78 1/-
vermilion .... Volume 3

Straits Settlements 1867 "2"
on 1½-on½-anna .... Page 123
Straits Settlements 1884 4¢-on-4¢-on-5¢
surcharge .... Volume 3
Straits Settlements 1899 5¢ missing
surcharge .... Page 125
Sweden 1855 3-skilling-banco color
error .... Volume 1
Sweden 1856-62 2-skilling-banco
local .... Volume 3
Sweden 1879 Tretio error .... Volume 2
Sweden 1891 5-ore brown ..... Page 127
Switzerland 1843 Double
Geneva .... Volume 1
Switzerland 1845 Basel Dove .... Volume 1
Switzerland 1849-50 Geneva
4 centimes .... Volume 2
Switzerland 1850 Rayons .... Volume 1
Switzerland 1878 5-centime
rayed-star due .... Volume 3
Switzerland 1882-99 5-centime
tete-beche .... Volume 3
Switzerland 1935-38 10-centime+15c
inverted surcharge .... Page 129
Tasmania 1853 4-penny Van Diemen's
Land .... Page 131
Tobago 1880 6-penny bisect ... Page 133
Togo 1914-15 occupation
issues .... Volume 1
Tonga 1897 7½-penny inverted
king .... Volume 2
Transvaal 1869 1-shilling tete-beche
pair .... Page 135
Trinidad 1847 Lady McLeod ..... Volume 1
Trinidad 1901 1-penny missing
value .... Volume 3
Turkey 1868 Asia Minor Steamship
locals .... Page 137
Turks Islands 1873 ½-penny-on-
1-shilling .... Page 139
Tuscany 1851-52 rarities .... Volume 2
Uganda 1895-96 typewritten
issues .... Volume 1
United States 1845 New Haven
provisional .... Volume 2
United States 1845 New York
provisional .... Volume 1
United States 1845 St. Louis
provisionals .... Volume 1
United States 1846 5¢ Brattleboro
provisional .... Volume 3
United States 1846 Alexandria
provisional .... Volume 1
United States 1846 Annapolis
provisionals .... Volume 1
United States 1846 Baltimore
provisionals .... Volume 1

166

United States 1846 Boscawen provisional	Volume 1
United States 1846 Lockport provisionals	Volume 1
United States 1846 Millbury provisionals	Volume 1
United States 1846 Providence provisionals	Volume 2
United States 1851 1¢ blue Franklin	Volume 2
United States 1857-61 5¢ Jefferson	Volume 2
United States 1857-61 90¢ blue	Volume 3
United States 1860 2¢ Beckman carrier	Page 141
United States 1861 August issues	Volume 2
United States 1867 1¢ Z grill	Volume 2
United States 1869 inverts	Volume 1
United States 1869 Running Chicken	Volume 1
United States 1870-71 24¢ grill	Volume 2
United States 1871 $500 Persian Rug	Volume 2
United States 1873 Buffalo Balloon	Volume 1
United States 1893 4¢ Columbian	Volume 2
United States 1894 Bicycle stamps	Volume 3
United States 1898 8¢ Trans-Miss imperf-between	Page 143
United States 1901 Pan American inverts	Volume 1
United States 1902 Full-Face McKinley postal card	Volume 2
United States 1906-08 Schermack perfs	Volume 3
United States 1908 coils	Page 147
United States 1909 4¢ and 8¢ bluish papers	Volume 3
United States 1911 3¢ Orangeburg coil	Volume 1
United States 1911 25¢ Vin Fiz	Volume 1
United States 1916-17 30¢ perf 10	Page 151
United States 1917 5¢ error cliche	Volume 1
United States 1918 24¢ inverted Jenny	Volume 1
United States 1923 Harding Memorial perf 11	Volume 3
United States 1930 2¢ Von Steuben imperf	Page 153
Uruguay 1858 180-centavo color error	Volume 2
Uruguay 1858 tete-beche pairs	Volume 1
Uruguay 1867 60-centavo Diligencia	Page 155
Uruguay 1895 25-centesimo inverted center	Page 158
Vancouver Island 1865 5¢ imperforate	Volume 2
Venezuela 1874 inverted frames	Page 161
Virgin Islands 1867-68 Missing Virgin	Volume 1
Western Australia 1879 2-penny color error	Volume 3

167